GANGS, GUNS & GOD

G.A.N.G. R.E.S.C.U.E.

Art Wilson

Gangs, Guns & God © 2024 Art Wilson

All rights reserved. No part of this publication may be reproduced or transmitted in any form or by any electronic or mechanical means including photo copying, recording, or any information storage and retrieval system now known or to be invented, without permission in writing from the publisher or the author.

Name: Wilson, Art
Title *Gangs, Guns & God* by Art Wilson
Interior and cover layouts: Robert Ousnamer

ISBN: 978-1-963611-57-1

Subjects: 1. Religion/Chiristian Living/Men's Interest
2. Religion/Christien Living/Missions

Unless otherwise noted, Scriptures are from The Holy Bible, English Standard Version® (ESV®)
© 2001 by Crossway, a publishing ministry of Good News Publishers. All rights reserved.

Published by EABooks Publishing
a division of Living Parables of Central Florida, Inc.
eabookspublishing.com

Acknowledgments and Dedications

I would like to acknowledge so many people who helped in my writing this book. Thank you to the Destin and Pensacola Word Weavers Chapters. I have been blessed to have numerous, talented, Christian writers who advised and encouraged me in this endeavor. I am grateful for Cheri and her wonderful team at EA Books Publishig—without their guidance, this book would have never been completed. Also, thank you to my awesome editor, Peter Lundell.

In addition, I want to dedicate the book to my wife, Vicky, who went through a lot of difficult years while I worked with the gangs in Chicago. She had many sleepless nights over the years, wondering if I would come home alive, and she held our family together. When people would ask her, "How could you let him go do a ministry that was so dangerous for so many years?" Her reply was always the same, "He doesn't belong to me; he belongs to God."

Over the years, many pastors, ministers, and friends encouraged me to write this book. The reason for my delay was because I was afraid the book would be about me rather than God. He alone is worthy of all honor, glory, and praise.

I hope this book is an encouragement to husbands, wives, parents, and grandparents to realize that if our mighty and loving God can save gang members, then there is no one so hard that He cannot reach. He is in the "life changing" business. Take heart. Keep praying. He is at work whether we see it or not.

Art Wilson

Director—G.A.N.G. R.E.S.C.U.E. Ministries

gangrescue@aol.com

GANGS, GUNS & GOD

G.A.N.G. R.E.S.C.U.E.

Art Wilson

Contents

Acknowledgements	i
Chapter 1	1
The Confrontation and Confirmation	
Chapter 2	12
The Parting	
Chapter 3	23
Saved By the Gangster Disciples	
Chapter 4	38
The Toughest Task I Ever Tried to Do	
Chapter 5	46
The Same Yesterday, Today, and Forever	
Photos	53
Chapter 6	65
Sent Out Two by Two	
Chapter 7	75
Gangs in Prisons	
Chapter 8	86
Locked Up but Free	
Chapter 9	95
The Angels Were Rejoicing	
Chapter 10	106
Emergency Call from Chicago	
EPILOGUE	114
About the Author	115

ivi

Chapter 1

The Confrontation and Confirmation

Sitting in the middle of Pilsen Park in one of Chicago's most dangerous and violent areas, I waited for a notorious gang called the Ambrose to come to talk with me. I was in a place known locally as "the hood" or "the projects." Everywhere I looked, graffiti marred the dilapidated buildings. This is how gangs mark their territories. Bullet holes covered the walls, revealing what a war zone the area is. On one of the park benches, a homeless man was asleep and snoring loudly. I wondered how many young men had been killed here. It all had a feeling of darkness, anger, hopelessness, and evil. A wave of sadness took over my emotions. I prayed that the Lord might use even me to help and offer hope to the gangs as well as those living on the streets. It seemed as if society had discarded and given up on them. The city had an "out of sight-out of mind" mentality. But I knew my Jesus didn't see them that way. There is no one He can't reach and change.

As I would learn over my many trips to Chicago, the enemy hates losing people or territories that belong to him. He would fight to hold on to them. The eerie environment was a world I had never entered before and had no experience with.

As the time approached for the gang to show up at our designated time, I began to doubt God's calling on my life to share the gospel with gang members. Questions flooded my mind, "Will I ever see my wife and children again? Did I hear from God, or am I just foolish and naïve?"

Out of fear and concern for my safety, our oldest daughter had said, "Dad, the Lord would never call you to leave your family and business and put your life in danger."

Then the gang members appeared in the distance. They were wearing what I had been told to look for, which was light blue and white clothing. As they got nearer, my heart started to race, my palms began to perspire, and my mouth felt like cotton. This gang's reputation in Chicago was frightening, especially if anyone came on their sacred territory or "turf," as they called it.

It is incredible how sharp a person's senses become when danger approaches. Everything around me seemed to come into more detailed focus. Used and discarded hypodermic needles from the drug addicts lay all over the ground. A pungent stench of urine, where the homeless relieved themselves each night, filled my nostrils. Discarded wine bottles littered the ground. Shirts and tennis shoes that were too dilapidated to wear any longer were also thrown away.

What would I say to these young men? How would I even start a conversation? I began to pray and remembered what the Lord had told me months earlier, "Tell them I love them and have a plan for their lives too. If only they will trust and obey Me."

Sweat dripped down my brow as about twenty young gang members entered the park. Pistols protruded from their belts. They seemed to take up predetermined positions like the military.

I found out earlier, through a contact on the telephone, the leader's name was Steven. He sat down next to me and cautiously looked me over. I extended my hand, hoping he would do the same. To my relief, we shook hands. My contact, who knew Steven and whom Steven trusted, told him I was okay and my only motivation for coming was to care about him and his gang.

Three gates led in and out of this park. Steven sent three young men to post themselves at each gate as lookouts. I asked him why they couldn't all join us to hear what I had to say. His reply caused me to break down right at that moment. God spoke to me through Steven as he said, "Art, we decided if you care enough about us to come in here by yourself and risk your life, if anyone is going to get to you, they'll have to go through us first."

All of the doubts and fears I felt earlier immediately disappeared. This response confirmed the call the Lord had placed on my life months before.

We all spent several hours that day talking, and I bought all the guys a burger and fries. As my grandmother used to say, "Food is great at bringing people together."

The various gang members had several different attitudes about me being there. Some were welcoming, some showed distrust, and others were angry about my presence. I'm glad their attitudes toward me improved over our days together.

I told Steven and his gang I was here, on this first trip, for a month and hoped to continue to meet with them two or three times each week. I gave each guy a New Testament and asked if they would read the Scriptures a little each day. Then we could discuss what they read.

It amazed me how God changed my heart toward gangs. Before He called me to this ministry, my wife, Vicky, reminded me about my past attitude toward them. I always thought, "They should get what they deserve." And, "Gangs need to be locked up, and throw away the key." The Lord had broken my heart for them, and I had a burden and love for them that defied explanation.

One day, after meeting and discussing God's Word, I was walking back to catch a cab. Suddenly, a strange and uncomfortable feeling came over me, like I was being followed. Nervously, I stopped to turn around and, sure enough, one of the young men was standing directly behind me. His street name was Silent. Without going into why he was called Silent, suffice it to say each member's street name had to do with what he did for the gang.

I asked, "Is there something I can do for you?"

His reply shocked me. "Art, I'm tired of this gang life and have been looking for a way out. Would you pray for me to change?"

Seeing the Holy Spirit moving in this young man's precious life was a blessing. I hugged him and said praying with him would be an honor. I put my hand on his shoulder, and we prayed together and discussed what he would need to do to get out of Chicago. Because of Silent's gang reputation, he and I both knew if he remained in the city, his life expectancy, most likely, wouldn't be very long. He said his family members living in another state would take him in.

I asked if he had started reading the New Testament I'd given him. He said he had not. Looking at verses in the Book of Romans, we went over the plan of salvation together.

I asked if he wanted to pray to receive Christ as his Savior, and we discussed what that meant. He understood it would not always be easy, but it was worth every sacrifice.

Silent said, "Yes, Art. I want to follow Jesus and be saved."

We prayed together on that street corner. What a blessing to be used by God. It was a humbling experience.

Silent said, "Now I finally have hope for my future."

"Yes, my friend," I replied. "Jesus promised to always be with us, through the hard times and the good."

This all took place in a violent and poverty-stricken Hispanic neighborhood called Pilsen. Silent had wanted to talk with me privately, away from the gang. These young men always feel the need to keep up a macho image while with their fellow gang members. Showing weakness or vulnerability can prove dangerous. To survive and earn respect, they have to maintain a persona of strength without showing any hesitation. This had become a learned behavior just to be able to survive in their violent gang culture. Silent is an excellent example that this persona is not who they truly are deep in their hearts.

After spending much of the day together, Silent and I parted ways. I encouraged him to grow in his faith by spending time in God's Word and prayer.

"I will," he promised.

Boarding the L-Train to return to my room, thoughts about what happened flooded me. Did I really pray with a Chicago gang member to receive Christ as his personal Savior? I was thankful that God even used me to witness such a powerful event. Silent's life would be changed forever. To God be the glory.

Before embarking on this trip to Chicago from our home in Niceville, Florida, the Lord revealed two verses in the Book of Ezekiel. They were my marching orders while attempting to carry out this His gang ministry. The scriptures are found in 2:6–7 which says, *"And you, son of man, do not be afraid of them, nor be afraid of their words, though briers and thorns are with you and you sit on scorpions. Be not be afraid of their words, nor be dismayed at their looks, for they are a rebellious house. And you shall speak my words to them, whether they hear or refuse to hear, for they are a rebellious house"* (ESV).

Verse six encourages us not to be afraid, while verse seven is a command to share the gospel. It is not a request. These scriptures also remind us that we are responsible for obeying the "telling." The results are not up to us. I suppose that command is valid for all of us, no matter what ministry the Lord might call us to. Peace and joy come from knowing Christ promises to be with us. God's Word is a reminder in John 15:5, *"...For apart from me you can do nothing"* (ESV).

Little did I know I would cling to these verses during this month in Chicago and on future trips.

Before leaving home, I heard and read about a place in the city where over fourteen thousand people lived. It was notorious for gangs, drugs, violence, and sensational crimes. One example was when two police officers were killed by a sniper from one of the project's high-rise buildings. Through constant gunfire, a gang known as the Gangster Disciples violently kept their hold on this area from other gangs. It had the reputation of being one of the worst and most violent places in Chicago—and in the entire country. I believe the Lord used my initial encounter with the Ambrose gang as a learning experience and preparation to enter this infamous and frightening place, Cabrini Green.

People from my hometown had heard of it and warned me not to go there. They read and heard that outsiders who enter the projects don't come out alive. I knew this was where the Lord called me to go and share the gospel.

That night I spent most of the evening praying for God to help me be bold and obey His calling. My prayers were also for His divine protection and guidance. The Lord has been so good to my family and me. Knowing that Jesus gave His all for me on the cross, how could I not give my all back to Him?

The next day, for the first time, I would walk into Cabrini Green to share the gospel with gang members and hopefully start building relationships.

Speaking with my wife, Vicky, on the telephone that night, I asked her to let our church know what was happening and to pray for me. I am so blessed to have a praying wife and church family because that is where the victory is won—on our knees.

I didn't sleep much that night and prayed, "Father, please help me to be faithful and obedient to your calling for Your honor and glory."

The next morning brought a beautiful and sunny day. Trying to eat a light breakfast, I had no appetite as I pondered my destination. The L-Train platform that would take me to Cabrini wasn't a long walk. Surprisingly, Moody Bible Institute wasn't far from the projects.

Boarding the train, I took my seat. Several people started conversing with me and asked," Where are you going this fine day?"

I replied, "I'm going to Cabrini Green to spend the day there."

They laughed and said, "No. Where are you going?"

They were Chicago residents and couldn't believe what I'd said. They repeated the exact words I heard in my hometown, "No outsider goes into Cabrini Green and comes out alive, especially if you are white. Do you not know the Black Gangster Disciples run it? You won't last five minutes in there." With that, our conversation ended. They must have thought I was either crazy or lying to them.

I wondered if this was the enemy's way of discouraging me from the mission the Lord called me to. God reminded me of Ezekiel 2:6–7, which gave me strength and encouragement.

The L-Train stopped at the destination nearest Cabrini. I got off and started walking. It was still about a mile away, but I could already see the numerous high-rises that make up the projects. The buildings known as the "reds" were seven, ten, and nineteen stories tall. The other buildings, called the "whites," were fifteen and sixteen stories. It was amazing how massive the place was. Pavement made up the floor of Cabrini, and as you walked in, the red buildings were on both the right and the left. Breezeways connected the buildings. In the center was a small children's playground that was barely standing. Rat and cockroach infestations were everywhere. Rotting and putrid garbage piled up trash chutes that looked like they had never been emptied. Electricity and water utilities were broken down, and graffiti was everywhere.

Getting closer, I first encountered the reds. A sizeable arch-shaped opening in the brick wall formed the entrance. And around it was graffiti and bullet holes in the walls, similar to what I had seen before where the Ambrose gang lived. All the dilapidated buildings looked as if they could fall at any time. The city didn't seem to care enough to keep them up.

As I got closer to the entrance, those words popped into my mind again, "Nobody goes into that area and comes out alive." It was apparent where those thoughts came from. Scram Satan, you lose.

It was time to enter the notorious Cabrini Green, which I had heard and read about for years. A movie was even made about it. I never dreamed my feet would touch the inside of such a place.

By the entrance were four young men covered in tattoos. They also had pistols and knives in their belts. One approached me and asked, "Do you know where you are? I wouldn't go in there if I were you."

Before this trip, I had researched the Gangster Disciples and knew their colors were black and blue. All four wore those same colors.

How would I make an impression on them? Then God gave me the answer. It was easy to notice that their sports equipment was in bad shape and wouldn't last much longer. Their basketball was falling apart, the old football they used was losing its outer covering, and they were throwing a baseball but had no gloves.

I said, "Guys, some of your sports equipment has seen better days. How about I get you some newer equipment and bring it back here?"

They laughed sarcastically, and one of the young men said, "Sure you will. Why would you do that for us?"

"Because I care about you and want to get to know you better."

They seemed taken aback by my response.

One of them said in a mocking tone, "Okay. We're sure we will see you later."

They all laughed again, confident they would never see me again.

Returning to the L-Train, I went to a sporting goods store I had seen a few days earlier and bought balls and gloves. Making it back to the train, I went to find the gang members I'd spoken with earlier.

Near where I last saw them, one young man yelled to the anothers, "You won't believe this. That dude did come back, and he's carrying a lot of stuff with him."

What a blessing to perform this small task for them. I learned early on these young gang members have had promises made to them and broken their entire lives. Most of their families had disintegrated either due to parents being incarcerated or killed. The gang culture was generational. The majority of gang members never knew who their "fathers" were, and most of the "mothers" abandoned them due to prostitution or drug addiction. If they had any family members left in their lives, it was usually a grandmother. Gangs take the place of families that no longer exist. It is a sad but sociological truth. It was easy to tell that keeping my word made some headway toward building relationships. Only God could orchestrate something like this.

Going to where I met them earlier, they invited me to enter their territory, which was a huge deal. One of the young men even brought over a chair for me to sit in. What a surprise. I was now inside Cabrini. Numerous used hypodermic needles lay on the children's playgrounds where drug deals had gone down. No one seemed to care for the safety of the little ones. Relationships and trust began to form, but I wasn't prepared to see and experience the violence and danger that would still come in a place where life meant nothing.

Chapter 2

The Parting

During my initial month in Chicago, I regularly met with Steven and his gang, except for a few who wanted nothing to do with me. Despite this, my relationships with the others grew stronger, as did the trust. Many guys even invited me into their apartments to meet their families. That was a true blessing for me.

Their tiny apartments were in rough condition and falling apart. I discovered the landlords couldn't or wouldn't spend the money to keep them up.

I met some incredible mothers, grandmothers, children, and grandchildren. For economic reasons, each family lived together in their crowded apartments. Even though they lived in horrible poverty, they were always ready to share with others what little they had. I learned so much about life from them. Many had four to a bed. Whenever a family had me over, they cooked a delicious meal for me. It was usually rice and beans, but it was a blessing just to be invited.

Most of the families living in these horrible conditions were never sure where their next meal would come from. Some would have nothing to eat for two or three days. The number of families who experienced this in Chicago was in the thousands. It broke my heart.

One day, as I talked with Steven and his girlfriend, Mary, they asked if I would be their son's godfather. What a blessing and surprise. "Of course. It would be an honor."

Another exciting event happened the following day. Steven, a few of his gang members, and I were having lunch in the park. Suddenly, about six police cars drove in with lights and sirens blaring. It turns out they were conducting a raid. They began grabbing several of the gang members and searching them. Two policemen approached me, and Steven yelled, "Leave him alone. He's with a church. Don't bother him."

The two officers hesitated and finally decided not to bother me. It was a very chaotic event. They told Steven and his gang to clean up their graffiti and left as fast as they came in.

This area, known as Pilsen, was mainly Hispanic and had one of the highest poverty rates in the entire city. One interesting fact about the small apartments Steven and the gang members and their families lived in was what hung on the inside of all the front doors. One item was a picture of a baby boy—the baby Jesus. Next to it in all the homes was a stem of garlic. Having both of these items hanging over their front doors showed they mixed superstition along with their religion. This had been passed down from generation to generation.

I asked Steven what the garlic was for. He said it was to ward off evil spirits. This reminded me of our pastor's sermon a couple of months earlier. The title of it was "Jesus plus nothing." The lesson's main point was, "Jesus is all we need. It isn't Jesus plus anything else." This was a great topic to discuss when we got together for the next Bible study in the park.

As I learned more that month, things between rival gangs were getting much worse and more violent, especially between the Ambrose, La Raza, Party Boys, Bishops, and Satan's Disciples. So many innocent people were dying in the crossfire between the gangs. A lot of the residents started sleeping on their floors to avoid being shot. Families would even take their babies from their cribs and lay them on floor mats in an effort to keep them under the gunfire. The number of innocent people being killed due to the gang wars was astronomical. Sadly, even small children playing in their yards were often unintended victims.

I went back to my room for some rest and to take a break the next day from constantly seeing and being with all the gangs, drug addicts, homeless, prostitutes, and drunks. As soon as I thought, "I need a break," the Lord reminded me that though I can take a break. They can't.

Feeling ashamed, I asked Jesus to forgive me and continue to break my heart for these precious people whom He went to the cross for too. I was reminded of 1 John 4:20: *"If anyone says, 'I love God,' and hates his brother, he is a liar; For he who does not love his brother whom he has seen cannot love God whom he has not seen"* (ESV).

Before returning to my room, I walked to the hardware store to buy a box fan for my sixth-floor window. There was no air conditioning, and June is a sweltering month in Chicago. To stay somewhat cool at night, I would take a cold shower or two down the hall to cool off and get some sleep. Raising the window, I placed the fan in the opening and let it back down until it was snug. Small openings were still on the sides since the window was larger than the fan. That would have to do for now.

Falling asleep with the light still on was a big mistake. I woke up covered with moths and other flying bugs. They were all over my clothes, my face, and the bed. That wasn't very smart. It took a couple of hours to get rid of all the bugs. I stuffed the sides of the window, where there were openings, with towels. Hopefully this will solve the problem.

The room also had no television. The Lord wanted to remove any distractions so my time would be focused on prayer and reading His Word. He also wanted me to go on this first trip by myself. God knows what we need and when we need it. The month was a blessed time of drawing closer to my heavenly Father. I wouldn't take anything for it.

One day while walking again in the Pilsen area of Chicago, I was fortunate enough to run into three pastors. The Lord had burdened their hearts too with this violent and unreached neighborhood. As we all know, there are no accidents with God. They invited me to their church, and worshiping with them was a blessing. One thing I have learned through this experience is that there is no one so hard-hearted God can't reach. I am an eyewitness to the fact that He can change a heart of stone to one of flesh. This is a great encouragement to anyone who has someone they care about who seems unreachable. If He can change the lives of gang members, the Lord can do the same for your loved ones.

Every night, I went to bed to the sounds of gunshots and sirens. Chicago was much different from my small town of Niceville, Florida. Also, on this scale, urban ministry differed greatly from anything I had done before. Over time, I began to get used to the sights and sounds around me.

The next day I was to pick up Steven to take him to lunch. One of the pastors I had met generously offered me his car to borrow any time I might need it.

Waking up to a beautiful but hot day, I drove to Steven's neighborhood. Carrying a newspaper, he got in the car.

"Good morning, my friend," I said. "Are you reading the paper to stay in touch with the news?"

"No, sir. We must drive through the turf of one of our rival gangs to get to where we're going. I brought the paper to hold up in front of my face. If they recognize me, we're done for."

That was some exciting news I hadn't planned on. As we started driving to our destination, my prayers were going up. By the grace of God, we made it past the other gang's turf and to the restaurant. What a ride.

Part of our lunch conversation was that Steven wanted out of the gang. His biggest concern was for the safety of his family. I said he could rely on me to help in any way I could. We began working on a plan. This would need to be carried out quietly and carefully. Getting in a gang requires prospects to either get jumped in (beaten), shot in the leg, or to kill a rival gang member. Getting out could be even worse. If a member tries to get out without permission, which is rare, the gang would kill that individual and possibly go after his family, too. We would have to get Steven and his family out quickly and cautiously. He would need to move far away beyond his reputation.

If I have learned anything so far on this trip, it is that the power and love of God can reach some of these gang members. Not all will accept and receive the gift of salvation, but some will. As God's people, we must go where they are and share the gospel. They are not going to walk into a church on their own. I'm not saying this type of ministry is for everyone, but for those He calls, it is a blessing.

After Steven and I had lunch, we drove back to his neighborhood and survived again going through the rival gang's territory.

My initial month in Chicago was coming to a close. I missed my family so much. After dropping off Steven and returning the pastor's car to him, I took the L-Train back to my room. As I approached the building, another person came toward me. His appearance was frightening. Tattoos completely covered his body as well as his face. When we neared each other, his first words caught me off guard, "Good evening, sir."

"Good evening to you, too," I replied.

"My name is Andre."

"My name is Art. It is nice to meet you."

He said his appearance was scary, but I shouldn't let that bother me. "Art, please let me share some of my testimony with you. May I ask if you are a follower of my Savior, Jesus Christ?"

I answered, "Yes, sir. I am."

He began telling me he had become a Christian while in prison. His calling was to try and reach those others might ignore or be uncomfortable with. The number "666" was tattooed on his hands. I became curious and asked him about it.

He said, "Art, in addition to being in prison, I was a Satan worshipper."

"Do you ever plan on trying to have those numbers removed?"

Andre wanted to keep the numbers despite what they represented. He thought the tattoo was part of his witness that God could change the heart of anyone.

I learned a lot from Andre. One thing was that it is important not to judge someone by how they look. Rather than hiding his past life, Andre used his past sins and mistakes to encourage others who had similar backgrounds. It can teach someone that Jesus forgives when we repent and turn to him. The Lord reminded me of Matthew 7:1-3 that says, "Judge not, that you be not judged. For with the judgment, you pronounce you will be judged, and with the measure you use it will be used to you. Why do you see the speck that is in your brother's eye, but do not notice the log that is in your own eye?" Before parting, we hugged and prayed for each other and the ministries the Lord had called us to.

After meeting Andre, I thought about the parable of the two sons found in Matthew 21: 28–32. In this parable, Jesus brings out mankind's hypocrisy and God's capacity to forgive the penitent who come to Him no matter their former status, condition, or circumstance. I asked the Lord to forgive me for judging others while I've had a "plank in my eye."

Returning to my room, I made plans for the next day. I wanted to see Steven and his gang again before returning home to assure them I would return in a month or two. It would hurt to leave because of the friendships and inroads made in Cabrini Green and Pilsen.

I went to Pilsen to see Steven and the Ambrose gang the next day. We met together and had a short Bible study. Before leaving, I prayed for them and their families. It was difficult parting because, in this environment, you never know who will still be alive when getting together again.

I returned to my building this time by walking part of the way and then taking the bus. While walking, I became disoriented and concluded I was lost. Trying to use landmarks didn't help either. After some time passed, I found myself walking down a street with a lot of commotion and yelling. Nearing the sounds, I saw numerous people cooling off and enjoying the water spraying from a fire hydrant. I couldn't decide whether to continue down the street where there were so many unknown people or backtrack and go in another direction.

Deciding this to be the shortest way back to my room, I kept walking.

Before leaving for Chicago, I studied the colors belonging to the various gangs. Getting nearer to where the crowd was, I suddenly froze. They were gang members belonging to the La Raza sect. It was easy to tell because they wore red, white, and green, the colors of the Mexican flag. Due to their bone-chilling reputation, I was told to be especially cautious if I ran into any of them.

I was too far down the street to go back. There must have been twenty-five or thirty gang members directly in my path.

Praying for God's protection, I continued walking. My legs felt like water, and my heart pounded as if it would beat out of my chest. It is hard to explain, but it was as if they didn't see me as I walked through the crowd. They parted and let me through without threats, yelling, or harassment. How could they not see me? It was indeed a miracle from God. They just continued what they were doing. I felt as if this was my "parting of the Red Sea" moment. God is so good. He still performs miracles, and is in control of everything. It was an event I would never forget. Those scriptures discussed earlier in Ezekiel 2:6–7 came to my mind where we are told three times not to be afraid, and once not to be terrified by them.

Returning to my room, I was exhausted. The stress of walking through the La Raza gang took its toll on me. I lay on my bed for a little rest but didn't wake up until the following day. It was time for me to pack and get to the airport.

The airplane took off on time with one stop in Atlanta. One more hour before I saw my wife and kids. On the second leg I looked at the beautiful clouds and reflected on all I had experienced that month. It seemed surreal.

Landing at the Destin/Fort Walton Beach Airport, it was hard to contain my emotions and not run past all the passengers to exit the plane. As I walked into the terminal, there they were. Crying and yelling, we ran to each other and embraced. Our little family was back together again.

We got in our car and drove home. After what I had seen in Chicago, the word home had an even more special meaning to me. I thought about everyone I had met and the poverty, anger, violence, hopelessness, and helplessness in which they lived. I recalled the constant gunfire and deaths of many young men and women involved in gang life. Why did the Lord allow me to live in our quiet town of Niceville, Florida? I vowed never to take any of it for granted.

My first night at home was tough. I didn't realize how much my experience in Chicago had affected me. Lying down, I couldn't sleep. My nerves were jumpy because it was so quiet. I finally got up and sat down on the patio outside.

Vicky joined me. "Are you okay?"

"No. I could jump out of my skin. There are no sirens, no gunshots, and no noise. I can't describe how I feel."

Vicky sat there with me most of the night, praying for me. I certainly didn't anticipate a reaction like this. As time passed, it got a little better.

Being busy in Chicago with the ministry, I hadn't thought much about how my trip would affect my family. I found out later that my children had a difficult time because their friends would overhear their parent's conversations. Things like, "I don't see how Art can survive his trip considering where he is going." Then their children, meaning no harm, would tell ours what their parents said. Of course, this would upset our kids greatly, and Vicky would have to calm them down. Hearing this broke my heart.

While talking with Vicky one evening, I noticed she looked pale and gaunt. I asked her if she was all right. She replied that everything was fine, but some friends told me she hadn't slept well while I was gone. They would ask her the same thing about how she was coping. Her answer was always the same, "I am fine." Vicky's best friend told me she only wanted to hold the family together, but it was hard for her to wonder each day what danger I might be in. She has always been my hero. Her love for the Lord has always inspired me.

When God calls us to a particular area of ministry, our families go along with us emotionally, if not physically. When our friends at church heard about where I would be going. Some asked, "You aren't going to let him go, are you, Vicky?"

Her response was always, "He doesn't belong to me. He belongs to God." That answer was a powerful testimony to her faith, leaving many speechless, including me.

Those two months I was home passed quickly. I strived to keep my business going and spend as much time as possible with Vicky and our children. My heart was with my family, but it was also with the gangs in Chicago. I wondered how many of those I had met would still be alive when I returned.

The time for me to return to Chicago was almost here. I prayed that the Lord would give my family strength and peace on this next trip.

Chapter 3

Saved By the Gangster Disciples

How did God's calling me to share the gospel with gangs start?

Coming from a nice small town in northwest Florida, appropriately and maybe humorously, called Niceville, no one ever expected me to become involved in something like this. Before living here, I was raised in a small town in Arkansas called Benton. The Lord must have a sense of humor sending someone like me to a major city like Chicago.

We have probably all heard the old saying, "Be careful what you pray for. God might give it to you." In my case, it was very accurate. For the previous few months, my prayers were the same ones Bob Pierce, the founder of World Vision, prayed.

That prayer is, "Let my heart be broken by the things that break the heart of God." One day, He took me up on it. Vicky reminded me how I disliked gangs and always said they should get what they have coming to them.

I dropped my kids off on a Friday morning at their elementary school. While driving to work, I had an experience that couldn't be explained or put into words. It caused me to pull over and turn off the engine.

As followers of Christ, I believe we have all sensed something and then felt something like, "Maybe that was a word from God." Then in some rare cases, at least for me, we might feel a powerful presence of the Lord that causes us to stop whatever we are doing. It is an experience we long to have again, putting us on our knees. At this moment, I felt that God was right there with me. In my spirit, I felt He was telling me He has a plan for young people involved in gangs and wants me to go to them where they live and tell them He loves them. They must hear the gospel and have a chance to accept it. He said He would be with me and protect me. Of course, I'm not saying these words are quotes from God; they are only what I felt in my spirit. Being a fairly conservative Christian, I wouldn't say I am an exceedingly spiritual person, and we aren't to base our faith on feelings. It must all line up with the Word of God. I tried to put into words, probably very poorly, the experience I had.

I continued sitting in my car, taking in what had just happened. Why would He use someone like me with no ministerial education and who grew up in a small town? Then I remembered who Jesus spent time with. There were no outcasts with Him. His birth was announced to the shepherds considered unclean due to their work with animals. The Gentiles were outcasts because they weren't Jewish. The woman at the well was looked down on because she was a Samaritan and had many husbands in the past. Everyone avoided the woman with the issue of blood because society called her unclean, as they did the lepers. The list goes on and on. I felt ashamed of my past attitude toward gangs, and the Lord immediately changed my heart. I went from detesting gang members to having a love and concern for them. There was no explanation except that God changed my heart immediately. I felt ashamed of my past mindset.

What would I say to my wife and kids about this new calling the Lord gave me? How would they accept this? It could radically change our lives.

I started the car and drove home. Walking into the house, I asked Vicky if we could sit down and talk about something.

I explained to her as best I could what had just transpired. Her reaction caught me by surprise.

She smiled and said this was an answer to her prayers.

Up to this point, my life consisted mainly of non-stop work. She said her prayers for me had been for God to use me in some ministry. This would help me draw nearer to Him rather than being engrossed in work.

I had no idea she had been praying that prayer for me. She didn't know that at the same time I had been praying the prayer that Bob Pierce prayed. Neither she nor I ever dreamed the Lord would call me to share the gospel with gangs. He answers prayers according to His perfect will and timing.

After Vicky and I talked, we began praying that God would show us the when and the where of His calling. We were to trust all the details into His mighty and loving hands.

After several weeks of fervent prayers, we agreed I was to go to a large inner city. The question was, which one? We considered New York, Los Angeles, San Francisco, Chicago, and Miami but had no peace or answer. So we continued to wrestle with this.

Then one evening, while having our weekly dinner at our church, we began reading the prayer requests distributed on the tables. One in particular caught our attention. A couple of our church members had a prayer request regarding their daughter. She had been going through a rebellious time and ran away to a large city. As time went on, she became involved in a gang. The name of the city was Chicago. The young lady had become the girlfriend of a gang leader there. His name was Steven. Also, she was coming home to Niceville the following weekend to visit her parents and get some of her belongings.

I told her parents everything going on in my life and the calling the Lord had given me. "Is it possible for me to spend a few minutes with her?" I asked.

They agreed. I was excited to be able to speak with her.

The weekend came, and I went to their home. Thanking the young lady for spending a few minutes with me, I began asking her some questions. It was easy to tell she was nervous and didn't want to go into much detail. Secrecy was a big part of the gang culture. She said, "Art, if I say too much and it gets back to the gang, my life could be in danger. I would suggest you don't go near any gangs in Chicago. You will probably never be heard from again if you do."

Oh my. What an encouraging conversation. As we continued to talk, she began to realize that my motive was only to get to know and help the gang in any way I could. She gave me Steven's telephone number and the general area they lived in.

This was God's answer to the where. It was also the first time Vicky and I had some small measure of peace.

As we continued to pray, we felt the Lord wanted me to go on this initial trip for a month. Narrowing down the best time to go, we felt July to be the correct month. It was now May, and things were coming together. Our desire was not to get ahead or behind the Lord's will for this, His ministry.

I am so blessed to have the wife God gave me. She supported and encouraged me in this, knowing that the unknown and the danger would take a toll on her and our children both now and in the future.

Now we needed to share with our kids what was coming up soon and what God had called their daddy to do.

***

Going back to Chicago the second time now, I would continue the gang ministry our Lord called me to.

It was difficult leaving my family again. We all cried and hugged at the airport. Our children clung to my legs, trying not to let me go. On this trip, they were more aware of where I was going and the danger involved. I felt guilt and remorse, but I knew this was what God called me to do. Through everything He would care for my family and grow them in their faith. We all prayed together, and I boarded the plane.

Many friends and family always asked why I would get involved in something so dangerous. My response was always that old saying, "Be careful what you pray for. God might give it to you." I suppose that is what happened to me. God is so worthy of our unconditional obedience. I only wanted to be found faithful for His honor and glory alone.

After the plane landed, I got to my room and called Vicky to tell her I made it. She mentioned something that confused both of us. "That was good how you held up that cross in the window on your plane. The kids liked it, too."

"I didn't hold up a cross. What are you talking about?"

This event has always been a mystery to us. We can only leave it at that. God is good.

I looked forward to returning to the Cabrini Green projects the next day. Continuing the relationships the Lord built on my previous trip would be awesome. I spent most of the evening in prayer for safety and guidance.

I woke up and took the train as near as it would take me to Cabrini. Walking the rest of the way, I came to the reds again. Upon entering the compound, I was welcomed by several of the young men I had met before.

As we sat down to talk, my heart broke to learn that two of my friends had been killed in a drive-by shooting. Sharing the gospel in this place became even more urgent to me.

During the week, I learned that each building has a lady who is in charge and lives in the building. In addition, another lady heads up the entire complex. Finding out who she was and where she lived, I set up an appointment to meet her.

The next day she and I met in their administrative room. She was kind and welcoming and even said word had gotten to her about what we had been doing for the residents. At the end of our discussion, she invited me to their next monthly meeting, which was that evening. This was where all the supervisory ladies came together to discuss how their buildings were doing. I was humbled and grateful to be invited and, of course, I said I would be there.

I returned to my room to rest before the meeting and catch up on writing in my daily journal. Having some time before I left, I began reading the Book of Psalms. The Lord took me to Psalm 121:7–8, which says, *"The Lord will keep you from all evil; he will keep your life. The Lord will keep your going out and your coming in from this time forth and forevermore"* (ESV). I needed those words as the gang violence continued to ramp up.

When I arrived at Cabrini to attend the meeting, I never expected what I walked into. Television cameras, news reporters, and radio media were entering the room. All the ladies living there had roped off an area around a large table for themselves. The media and reporters were to stay on the other side of the rope. When the ladies saw me come in, they yelled and motioned for me to sit with them. They were making bologna sandwiches for themselves and made one for me. I felt so grateful that they would include me as their friend.

Walking past the media and cameras with U.S. News and World Report and local Chicago media, I thought, "This must be a big deal."

I asked what was going on. One of the ladies said, "The mayor has been promoting his 'City Beautification' agenda. He wants to eventually tear down Cabrini Green and replace it with 'affordable housing' for us. We all know that whatever he replaces our buildings with, it will be out of our price range."

The meeting between the ladies and some of the council members was contentious. The press kept asking who I was, and the ladies replied, "He is our friend and has been helping our neighborhood. Leave him alone."

As bad as Cabrini is, the residents still felt that it was their home.

The meeting ended, and another date was set for the next one. I was asked if I would attend that one too. Of course! I gladly and humbly accepted their kind invitation.

Leaving the building, I noticed something that had never gotten my attention before. Most of the people living in the projects were women, children, and young gang members. Almost no fathers were living there to complete the family unit. No older men. I thought back to my school days in sociology when we discussed the importance of the nuclear family. That family comprised a mother, a father, and children living together as one social unit. This was rare or non-existent in the projects, which is where a lot of the young gang members' anger came from. As we all know, God created the family unit, which is very important to Him. He intended for men (fathers and husbands) to be godly leaders in their homes and communities. The man was to work and provide for his family as well as offer protection and love. Since most men in this environment abandoned their families and responsibilities, it caused a lot of anger and resentment to spring up. Hence, the number of gangs multiplied as they sought to be a part of some type of social "family." But this kind of family was never God's intention.

***

Chicago has representatives for each area of the city. These government officials are called Aldermen. I wanted to meet the one whose jurisdiction included Cabrini. After doing some research, I found his name and office address, and I set up a meeting for the following day.

The next morning, I took the city bus to his office. His secretary introduced us, and we had an excellent conversation. It turned out he himself grew up in Cabrini Green and wanted to help the people there any way he could. He even had his secretary type a letter on his letterhead stating he supported my ministry. He said, "Art, let me know anything you guys need." God's hand was obviously in all of this.

The following week, as I was walking on the outskirts of the projects about to go in, a car gunned its engine. Suddenly, it peeled out and sped directly toward me. This can't be good, I thought. Possible scenarios raced through my confused mind as the automobile got closer. Thoughts of my family engulfed me, and a sickening feeling of nausea, panic, and confusion took over my body. I prayed, "Lord, is this the end of my life? If it is, please take care of Vicky and the kids."

The car screeched to a halt next to me. The young men in the vehicle got out. They yelled at me to hurry and get in. I knew most of them and thought, What have I done to cause this?

After shoving me in the car, they jumped in. We took off, tires screeching, and sped away. By this time, my entire body was soaked with sweat. My thoughts raced back and forth. I pictured my wife and children at my funeral crying, and all they would have to endure. Other than doing drive-by shootings, another way gangs killed people was by kidnapping them in a vehicle, driving the victim out of the city, and killing them in a field somewhere. The body would be found some time later. Would this scenario be my end?

Driving a short distance, the car came to an abrupt stop.

"You can get out now, Art," one of the young men said.

By this time, I was perspiring profusely from fear, and my legs would barely hold me up.

I asked, "What was that all about?"

"We found out a drive-by was about to go down where you were walking, and we didn't want you to get hurt." As suddenly as they appeared, they took off.

I lost it right then and there. The fear, stress, and shock had worn me out. It took me a while to process what had occurred. The Gangster Disciples, one of Chicago's most feared and notorious gangs, cared enough to protect me. It was all so surreal. I felt as if I were watching a movie.

Walking back to the train platform, Romans 8:28 came to my mind. *"And we know that for those who love God all things work together for good, for those who are called according to His purpose"* (ESV). Returning to my room, I thanked the Lord for His love, mercy, and protection after that harrowing experience. There is only one who is good, and He is God.

I needed to have my quiet prayer time and Bible reading. Sitting on my bed, I went to Romans 10:14–15, *"How then will they call on him in whom they have not believed? And how are they to believe in him of whom they have never heard? And how are they to hear without someone preaching? And how are they to preach unless they are sent? As it is written, "How beautiful are the feet of those who preach the good news!"* (ESV).

I read these verses many times, but they now had a particular urgency in this environment.

It is rare for gang members in our large inner cities to live past there twenties. Whether they accept or reject the gospel, they must hear it. Those verses are why I am here. I prayed that the Lord would find me faithful and obedient in carrying out this mission. It certainly can't be done in my strength or ability, but the Lord promised to always be with us.

The next day, I was to meet with a young man who lived in Cabrini and wanted to talk with me privately. He was a huge guy and looked like a bodybuilder. Everyone called him Arnold because he was built like the actor Arnold Schwarzenegger. His real name was Quashay.

His size and demeanor didn't go together. Despite his intimidating presence, he had an aura that was gentle and quiet. Quashay was one of the young men I had met at the entrance to Cabrini my first time there.

He started the conversation by saying, "Art, I have heard you talking about this Jesus and would like to know more about Him. If he is such a big deal, why has nobody else come out of these churches to tell us about Him?"

Those words hit me hard and broke my heart. How was I to answer a question like that?

I decided to read some Bible verses to him, which say much more than I ever could about the

Lord's love and plans for Quashay's life. The Holy Spirit was at work drawing this young man to Him. We read many scriptures together because God's Word is powerful and life changing. One verse we read was Romans 1:16, *"For I am not ashamed of the gospel, for it is the power of God for salvation to everyone who believes, to the Jew first and also to the Greek"* (ESV). We continued by reading about what a person must do to be saved in Romans 10:9–10, which says, *"If you declare with your mouth, "Jesus is Lord," and believe in your heart that God raised Him from the dead, you will be saved. For it is with your heart that you believe and are justified, and it is with your mouth that you profess your faith and are saved."*

Quashay said, "Art, I believe and want to accept Jesus as my Savior."

What a thrill to hear this young man say those precious words.

We prayed together, and Quashay knelt beside the bench as we did. It was a very moving experience, and one I will always cherish and give thanks for.

I told him he had just caused a party to happen in heaven. "Quashay, Luke 15:10 says, *"Just so, I tell you, there is joy before the angels of God over one sinner who repents"* (ESV).

Quashay and I hugged. I told him to be sure to stay in prayer and the reading of God's Word I had given him. I said, "Quashay, I am so proud of you. Stand firm in your faith through both the good and the hard times. Jesus said He will never leave or forsake us. I promise to stand with you as you grow in your walk with Him."

A wonderful victory had been won, showing how valuable we are to God.

Before we parted, I asked Quashay if we could walk around Cabrini so he could give me some insight into the past history of the projects. As we began our tour, he pointed to the heavy metal grates installed recently. They were there to cover the open breezeways connecting each building.

He said, "Those grates were added because sometimes the drug dealers would come to collect their money. If the people didn't pay what was owed, they would toss the user's babies and children off the breezeways, killing them on the pavement below. The city finally came and installed the grates.

Hearing this made me sick to my stomach. I couldn't fathom such evil and disregard for life. The longer I stayed in the projects of Chicago, the more convinced I became that the struggle was spiritual. The enemy fights not to give up people or territory that belongs to him.

Ephesians 6:12 reminds us, *"For we do not wrestle against flesh and blood, but against the rulers, against the authorities, against the cosmic powers over this present darkness, against the spiritual forces of evil in the heavenly places"* (ESV).

***

I saw this tangibly on my next trip to Chicago. A good friend and member of our church told me he felt called to this ministry. He desired to go with me when I returned. I had never taken anyone with me before, and it made me somewhat nervous to be responsible for someone else. But if the Lord called him, who was I to interfere?

My friend Tommy and I flew into Midway Airport, the one I used most to Chicago. We arrived early in the day, so I took him to Moody Bible Institute to show him around. We purchased some Bibles and toured memorabilia and history about D. L. Moody and the Great Chicago Fire.

After leaving there, we took the city bus to our room to check in and empty our suitcases. Then we took the L-Train to Cabrini.

Before going in, Tommy and I prayed for protection and that the Lord might give us opportunities for spiritual conversations. I wanted to introduce him to some of the young gang members I had met on previous trips.

We approached the arched doorway to enter the projects. Suddenly, to my shock and amazement, Tommy was doubled over in pain.

"Tommy, what is wrong? Are you okay?"

"Art, I can't straighten up. I don't understand what is happening to me. The only way to describe it is that I feel there is evil around this place. It's as if an evil spirit is angry with me."

I didn't know what to do. I had never experienced this. All I could think of was to lay my hands on him and pray the blood of Jesus over his body. Tommy had never experienced anything like this either. As we continued to pray, he could eventually stand erect again without any pain.

We returned to our room to be sure he was still okay. I was reminded, again, about Ephesians 6:12, that our struggle is not with flesh and blood but with the spiritual forces of evil. We learned a lot that day, especially that the enemy didn't want us infringing on his territory.

Tommy stayed with me for several more days and then needed to return to his business. While there, I introduced him to several young gang members who had prayed to receive Christ as their Savior.

He said, "Art, I will be back."

Chapter 4

The Toughest Task I Ever Tried to Do

I found that Steven was right in warning me about how much worse the gang violence had gotten. Gunfire was more frequent. The news reported large numbers of people being killed daily in the crossfire of the gang wars.

I decided to write a letter to my eleven-year-old son, Buddy, in case something happened to me.

That night in my room, I began the letter by telling him Dad went home to be with Jesus. He would need to be the man of the house from this point forward. I'm ashamed to say I failed to finish the letter. While writing, I began to feel sick and ran to the bathroom to throw up. No matter how hard I tried, I could not finish it. It was the most difficult task I had ever attempted. Going to bed that night, I felt like a terrible failure.

Walking through Cabrini the next day, a lady ran up and said, "Art, you must come with me. A friend of mine's grandson was just shot and killed."

Following her to the grandmother's apartment, I asked how it happened. She said, "You won't believe this, but it resulted from an argument over a Snickers candy bar."

Wow. A precious life is gone because of a fight over a candy bar.

How can life in these projects be so insignificant? How can people become so callous and hard-hearted? The answer was very obvious. Satan was having his way in Cabrini and other projects throughout our country. We must go and get in the battle for these precious and hurting souls. Too many lives had been snuffed out early and too many hearts had been broken. The scriptures remind us that the cross is foolishness to those who are perishing, but we know Who has the power to turn it all around. We must go, not with a spirit of fear, but with a spirit of power, love, and self-discipline. Not in our own power, but in the power of Christ, our Savior, with the life-changing power of the gospel.

As we walked into the apartment, the grandmother was sitting there, distraught beyond words. Tears ran down her face, and she was shaking. She looked to be in her eighties.

Kneeling beside her, I asked if I could pray for God to give her strength, comfort, and peace.

She said, "Please pray for me. I'm a Christian, but I am hurting so bad."

Holding her hands, we prayed together for quite some time. It was such a privilege to be allowed to pray with this precious lady. She showed me photographs of her grandson and talked about the stories that went with them.

When we finished, she said, "Thank you so much, pastor."

"Ma'am, I am not a pastor, but I'm grateful to be able to pray with you."

We hugged, and she kissed me on the forehead. I promised to come back and check on her.

Inner city ministry is unique because you never know what you'll run into next. Many of the homeless living on the street have mental illnesses. They should be in a hospital receiving treatment. I have had people come up to me demanding money. Others have run up and started screaming and cursing at me. Often, some have even gotten in my face and began to chant some kind of gibberish. The days are never boring spending time in the "hood" of a large city like Chicago. I always pray that the Lord would show me how to handle each situation I come up against, and that I would show His love to everyone.

I know it sounds crazy, but being on these streets and in the projects was where I found the most peace and inner joy. That probably makes no sense. It doesn't to me either. When God calls us to a ministry, we experience difficulty, of course, but it doesn't compare to the blessing of seeing someone accept Jesus as his or her Lord and Savior.

***

It was Sunday morning, and I wanted to attend the service at a small church near where I was staying. I got ready and began walking, looking forward to worshipping and being able to hear the message.

Between my room and the church was a McDonald's restaurant. Passing the restaurant, a lady approached me and asked, "May I have some money for something to eat?"

Knowing how the streets worked, I wanted to be sure she wouldn't use the money for drugs or alcohol. "I would happily buy you something to eat.

Let's go to this McDonald's, and I will pay for whatever you want."

She proceeded to yell and curse at me. I guess she wasn't very hungry.

Continuing my walk to the church, I wouldn't let that incident affect my time in God's house. I arrived, and the people greeted me warmly. Like my room, the church was in a rough and poor neighborhood.

As I took my seat, people continued to file in. Many were members and regular attendees. Sometimes a person who appeared to be homeless would come in. The clothing they wore was torn and dirty. At one point, a young lady came in dressed very scantily with makeup smeared on her face. It looked like she had been crying.

Looking around, I thought, This is a church where you might expect to find Jesus.

The service began, and the worship music was wonderful. The pastor delivered a powerful message full of scriptures, encouragement, and truth. In the end, he gave an invitation.

The scantily dressed young lady went forward and cried while she knelt to pray. Due to how she was dressed, it left little to the imagination.

Rather than being upset, offended, or judgmental, two ladies who were church members went to where she was. They kindly covered her with a blanket as they knelt on each side of her. Then they put their arms around the young lady and prayed with her. It was one of the most beautiful acts I had ever seen. Watching this happen was a strong lesson in itself, without any words.

Later I was told the girl was a prostitute. The story of Rahab, in God's Word, came to mind. She was a prostitute the Lord used in His plans for the Israelites. Joshua sent out two spies, and Rahab hid them for their safety. She went from being a pagan prostitute to a heroine of the faith. She also left a life of shame to become a wife and mother. From Rahab would come the line of David, and she would be part of the lineage of Jesus.

I asked the Lord to help me to see people the way He sees them.

One night, while sleeping in my room in Chicago, the Lord woke me up. In my spirit, He gave me the name of His ministry. It was to be called GANG RESCUE. GANG would be an acronym for "Gangs Also Need God." RESCUE would be an acronym for "Reach Every Single Child Upon Earth."

Many in the gangs are young teenagers whose families disintegrated because of violence, drugs, and alcohol. Some have never known who their fathers are. This causes a lot of anger and low self-esteem. The gangs take the place of non-existent families. Sadly, in our country today, they can't build juvenile detention facilities fast enough to take care of the needs.

***

As the years and trips to Chicago passed, God began calling other people to accompany me.

I was in Cabrini again, and some of the gang members I knew were looking for me. They told me that Quashay, the muscular young man nicknamed Arnold, who was saved a few weeks earlier, had something to tell me. Hearing he had been taken to the emergency room, I was eager to see how he was doing.

I went to his apartment and found him there with a large bandage on his hand. He invited me in to talk.

"Art, I wanted to tell you what happened so you wouldn't think bad of me. You might have heard I got into a fight. It's important to me that you know I didn't start it. Three guys jumped me, and I was only defending myself. I knocked out all three, protecting myself. When I prayed to receive Jesus as my Savior, I was serious. One of the guy's teeth broke off and was embedded in my knuckles. It became infected. That's why I had to go to the hospital. I was never arrested and didn't want you to think bad of me."

Wow. His main concern was what I thought of him and his relationship with Jesus. He continued, "When I prayed that prayer with you about a month ago, I meant it. The Lord truly changed me, and I'm not returning to who I was."

What a humbling experience to hear those words from this young man as he confirmed his commitment to the Lord.

"Quashay, I could never think less of you and am so proud. Can I have a hug?"

We embraced, and I prayed for his hand to heal and his faith to grow and mature. As we parted, my heart was full and grateful. What a mighty God we serve.

We started some additional Bible studies in Cabrini each day. Some were for the women, some for the children, and some for the gang members. I was always surprised by the large numbers that would show up. It was an honor to share God's Word in this place. The enemy was losing ground, and he certainly didn't like it.

I debated whether to tell the following story. It reminds us that we are in a spiritual battle for souls. The story will sound quite bizarre and is certainly not something I am used to. Please give me grace about this true event. You never know what you might encounter on the mission field.

One afternoon as I walked back to my building, I saw something that gave me chills and made the hair on my neck and arms stand up. Rounding the corner of my building, his appearance was horrifying, as was his voice. His eyes were all black. There was no white or color. He couldn't have seen me coming because the building was all concrete. It was as if he could see me through the building and waited for me to come around the corner. Crowds of people walked on the sidewalk on both sides of us, but no one seemed to see him except me. His voice was deep and sounded like an echo as he said, "Stay off my turf, or you will wish you had."

I began praying for Jesus to protect and be with me. I looked away for a moment. Then he was gone.

Anyone who knows me knows I am a very conservative Christian and am not accustomed to seeing or sharing anything like this. If it seems nuts to you, I certainly don't blame you. It seemed nuts to me too. But it was real. And it seemed that perhaps a demonic person or manifestation finally confronted me after I had been doing so much on what was a playground of Satan.

After trying to collect my wits about me, I started back to my room. The people at the front desk asked, "Are you okay, Art? You look a bit flushed."

I nodded and got on the elevator. I entered my room and sat on my bed. It was difficult to take in what just happened.

The good news is that though we will go through battles in this life, we read the end of the book and are sure that God has won the war. I clung to the verse in 2 Timothy 1:7, which says that *"God gave us a spirit not of fear but of power and love and self-control"* (ESV). We can all rest and have peace in that promise.

Chapter 5

The Same Yesterday, Today, and Forever

As God began calling others to accompany me on some of my trips to Chicago, this enabled us to schedule a large cookout for the Cabrini Green residents. We needed to continue building relationships in the projects.

Approximately ten folks committed to the next trip, and we began making plans. It would be a massive undertaking since thousands lived there. The goal was to show Christ's love to the residents.

We decided to rent a large U-Haul and a massive grill to cook hotdogs and hamburgers. Two of our volunteers would drive the grill and the many donations all the way from Florida to Chicago, and everyone else would fly. Since everything was free, we got permission from the city.

My biggest concern was that we might not have enough food for everyone who might come. We would also need to get chips, cookies, and drinks. I believed that God would provide everything, so we went in faith.

Everyone arrived safely, and we went to our rooms to rest and pray that the Lord would be glorified in the event the next day—and that we would have safety and protection.

The next morning, we all headed to Cabrini. As we entered the compound, the people closely watched what was happening. I knew many of the folks but didn't know them all.

With all the tables set up, several of us were about to walk to the grocery store to purchase the food and drinks.

As we began to walk, a huge refrigerator truck pulled up next to us. Men started unloading food and drinks. A couple of us approached the workers and the truck and said, "Gentlemen, we didn't order anything. This must be for someone else."

One man returned to the truck and pulled out a work order. He read what it said: "This is from the residents of Cabrini Green and the City of Chicago for Gang Rescue Ministries. Thank you for caring."

All of us were shocked. Speechless. Tears welled up in everyone's eyes. We felt as if we were experiencing the feeding of the five thousand in Matthew 14:13–21. These verses say,

Now when Jesus heard this, he withdrew from there in a boat to a desolate place by himself. But when the crowds heard it, they followed him on foot from the towns. When he went ashore he saw a great crowd, and he had compassion on them and healed their sick.

Now when it was evening, the disciples came to him and said, "This is a desolate place, and the day is now over; send the crowds away to go into the villages and buy food for themselves."

But Jesus said, "They need not go away; you give them something to eat."

They said to him, "We have only five loaves here and two fish."

And he said, "Bring them here to me." Then he ordered the crowds to sit down on the grass, and taking the five loaves and the two fish, he looked up to heaven and said a blessing. Then he broke the loaves and gave them to the disciples, and the disciples gave them to the crowds. And they all ate and were satisfied. And they took up twelve baskets full of broken pieces left over. And those who ate were about five thousand men, besides women and children. (ESV)

We were so blessed and fortunate to see this again but in a different way. We discussed Hebrews 13:8, *"Jesus Christ is the same yesterday and today and forever"* (ESV) None of us would ever forget that experience.

Everyone who came to the cookout was fed. No one counted the people, but it was several thousand, and food was left over. What did the entire event cost the ministry? Nothing. The Lord provided as He always does. What a mighty God we serve.

New relationships were formed there in Cabrini. Our wonderful volunteers even prayed with some to receive Christ as their Savior.

By then we had been going to Chicago regularly for several years. Somehow, word had gotten out to various ministries and press organizations about how we had been working with gangs in Chicago. We certainly were not doing it for fame or notoriety. It was a calling.

One day, we were contacted by Moody Bible Institute to come and speak on their worldwide radio station. The name of the program is called Words to Live By. We had no idea how they heard of what our ministry was doing. It was an honor to share how the Lord changed the lives of some of the most hard-hearted gang members in the country. There is no one in our world whom Jesus can't reach. I prayed this would give people hope and encouragement regarding their loved ones who seemed unreachable.

After this, one of our volunteers showed me an article in the Promise Keepers periodical about Gang Rescue and the work being done in the well-known Cabrini Green projects. Again, we had no idea how they heard of the ministry.

A short time later, RBC Ministries' (now called Our Daily Bread Ministries) radio division sent out two men who wanted to go with us as we spoke with gang members in Cabrini. I asked how they heard about what the Lord was doing. They said they read the Promise Keeper article and wanted to see it themselves. Gangs have become a big topic all over the country.

We met them as they got off the L-Train. One of them, Bob, had been here with me before. Together we prayed for God's protection, guidance, and opportunities for spiritual conversations. We never entered Cabrini without praying first.

I had no idea they would bring a large microphone as we walked around and spoke to some of the gang members. They wanted to record the conversations we had. This concerned me because I wasn't sure how it would be received.

The four of us walked in. I wanted to go to a building I hadn't spent much time in. There were two gang members standing guard at the building's entrance. They took a defensive posture as we walked up to where they were, not knowing our intentions. I didn't know them, which was also concerning.

The young men became jumpy and on the ready as we got nearer. There were two strikes against us. One was because there were four of us. The other was the microphone, which, I could tell, made them nervous.

I asked Bob, one of our regular ministry volunteers, if he and one of the RBC men would mind stepping away for now so only two of us would be speaking with them. They agreed it was a good idea.

As we moved closer, things seemed a little less tense. I introduced myself and Dan with the Christian radio ministry.

One of the young gang members said, "We've heard about you, Art, and that you guys have been helping some of our people in here. You guys are the church people, right?"

Those words made me feel more at ease. Their guard seemed to come down quite a bit.

I asked, "Would you guys mind talking for a few minutes?"

One of the young men responded, "I guess not. What's that microphone for?"

Dan told them his radio ministry was doing a story about how our ministry might be making a difference for the residents and gang members living in Cabrini.

The other young man said, "I don't know. At least they care enough to come in here and risk their lives. Them just showing up is a big deal. We respect that. Nobody ever comes in here that doesn't live here. I don't want my name mentioned on your radio show."

Dan assured them both that no names would be mentioned.

We talked for several minutes. They had come to our cookout and appreciated that. Before leaving, I asked, "Do you guys mind if we give you each a Bible?"

One took one, and the other said, "No thanks."

I told them about our weekly Bible study in Cabrini and where we met.

"I hope you guys will join us sometime," I said. "Let me ask you one more question. Do you mind if we pray for you and your family before we go?"

One of the young men said, "No thanks," and walked back into the building.

The other said, "I don't want any prayers for myself, but my little brother is following what I do and just got locked up. And my grandmother has cancer and isn't doing good. You can pray for them."

"May I pray for them right now?"

"I guess so."

As we prayed, Dan and I put our hands on his shoulders.

When we finished, Dan said, "Can we get a hug?" And we had an awesome three-man hug. I told him we would see him again soon. We needed to follow up on what happened today.

"That would be okay."

We found Bob and the other gentleman, and Dan said, "This ministry is the real deal. I will tell you all about it later. Art, your ministry is very unique and a true blessing."

Whenever someone says something like that, I reply, "Thanks, but it isn't my ministry. I'm just grateful that I am allowed to work in God's ministry. All glory and honor to Him."

This is not false humility, as some might call it. This is the truth and why I waited so long to write this book. I didn't want it to be about me and feared it might be. We wanted it to be about our awesome God and what He did, not me or anyone else.

Photos

Photo 1: The "reds" – Cabrini Green – Chicago, Illinois. June 1998

Photo 2: The "whites" – Cabrini Green – Chicago, Illinois. July 1999

Photo 3: The "reds" – Cabrini Green – Chicago, Illinois. June 1997

Photo 4: The "whites" – Cabrini Green – Chicago, Illinois. August 2000

Photo 5: The "reds" – Cabrini Green – Chicago, Illinois. June 1999

Photo 6: Art & Head Resident of Cabrini Green – Chicago, Illinois. June 1997

Photo 7: Car parked by Cabrini Green – Chicago, Illinois. October 2000

Photo 8: The "reds" – Cabrini Green – Chicago, Illinois. May 2001

Photo 9: Cabrini Green gang member – prayed to receive Christ – Chicago, Illinois. July 2004

Photo 10: Children – residents of Cabrini Green praying to receive Christ – Chicago, Illinois. July 2002

Photo 11: Art with a Crip gang member – prayed to receive Christ – Chicago, Illinois. August 2003

Photo 12: Preparing for cookout in Cabrini Green – Chicago, Illinois. June 2001

Photo 13: The "reds" – Cabrini Green – Chicago, Illinois. June 2001

Photo 14: The "whites" – Cabrini Green – Chicago, Illinois. July 2002

Photo 15: One of the "whites" – Cabrini Green – Chicago, Illinois. April 2004

Photo 16: Incarcerated young inmate being baptized – Crestview, Florida. July 2007

Photo 17: Young inmates helping build house for Habitat for Humanity – Florida. July 2003

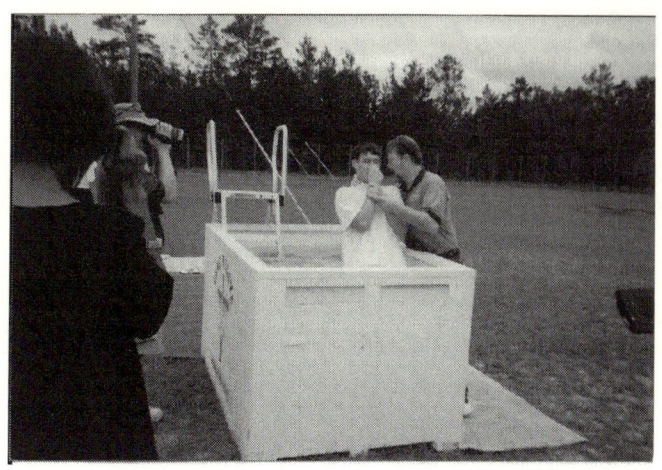

Photo 18: Another young inmate being baptized – Crestview, Florida. July 2007

Photo 19: Young inmates helping build Habitat for Humanity house – Florida. July 2003

Chapter 6

Sent Out Two by Two

On the next trip to Chicago, several pastors told me about a suburb nearby, which was well known as a violent gang area. To their knowledge, no one had ever gone there to share the gospel due to its dangerous reputation.

They also told me about a man who had wanted and felt called to go and tell the gang members living there about Jesus. Sadly, no one ever volunteered to go in there with him. He always wanted to pull his large grill behind his truck to offer food to break the ice, but to be effective, he needed another person to accompany him.

His name was Jimmy, and my pastor friends gave me his telephone number.

After much prayer, I felt the Lord would let me go with him.

The next morning, I called Jimmy and introduced myself to him. Since he knew the pastors who referred me, mentioning their names helped with a measure of credibility.

I said, "Jimmy, it would be an honor to go with you on this ministry the Lord has laid on your heart. If you will have me, I will be happy to assist you in any way."

"Art, I have been praying for the Lord to send me a brother in Christ to help. You are an answer to prayer."

We made plans and set a date to meet at his house the following Friday.

A lot of prayers were lifted in preparation for that day. Jimmy told me about the extreme gang violence in the neighborhood. He went on to say the gangs controlled the entire area. We would be going into streets where it wasn't advisable to enter if you didn't live there.

I said, "Jimmy, as you know, Jesus went to the cross for them too. They deserve to hear the good news and know His love for them. I am grateful for you allowing me to go with you."

Friday came, and I took a Chicago Transit Authority bus to Jimmy's house. He came out, shook my hand, and hugged me.

After praying together, we loaded the hotdogs, hamburgers, and other things into the back of his truck. Then we headed out to this "unreached" and violent suburb. I was somewhat nervous but excited to see what the Lord would do.

As we got closer to our destination, Jimmy said," There it is. The neighborhood starts right here."

It reminded me of where Steven and the Ambrose gang lived in the Pilsen area of Chicago. Horrible poverty was evident everywhere. A homeless man was rummaging through a trashcan to try and find something to eat. An elderly lady was limping while pushing a shopping cart that contained everything she owned. We noticed another elderly man's face full of wrinkles and looking like leather due to living most of his life in the sun and the elements. Children were running and playing barefoot amid broken glass and used hypodermic needles discarded by drug addicts. You could feel the hopelessness, helplessness, and anger of those who lived there. Bullet holes and graffiti covered every building. RIP, "Rest in Peace," was written on many of the walls. Under those letters were the names of gang members who had been killed.

Jimmy pulled his truck with the grill into a park. We both got out. He started getting the fire going as I unloaded the truck.

I could see some of the "scouts" checking us out from a distance. These were normally the youngest gang members stationed at the boundaries of where that gang's territory began and ended. The reason gangs use the youngest for that task is because if they get caught by the police, their sentences would be shorter due to their young age as juveniles.

There are several ways gangs initiate young men wanting to join. One way is by getting "jumped in," or beaten, by the gang members for a certain period of time. If they survive and don't run, they are accepted.

Another initiation rite is to kill a rival gang member. If this is done, they are in.

A third way is to allow a gang member to shoot them in the leg. Yes, it's crazy.

After Jimmy and I got the grill going, we started cooking the hotdogs and hamburgers. I had brought along a case of New Testaments. We at least wanted to get God's life-changing Word into some of the resident's hands.

We had been there about ten minutes when some gang members started walking toward us. When they got to where we were, one, who seemed to be the leader, said, "What are you doing here? This is our turf.

You ain't welcome here. You'd better pack up and leave while you still can."

Not a very warm welcome. Early in the ministry, the Lord taught me that walking up to gang members accomplished two things. First, it caught them off guard because it wasn't what they expected. Second, the very audacity of doing so caused a certain level of respect.

I walked up to the young man who threatened us, extended my hand, and hoped for a handshake. It didn't happen. Then I said, "We just wanted to come today and prepare some food for you and your families. Our only desire is to serve you all and hopefully build friendships. Do you prefer a hotdog or a hamburger?"

The response confused him for a minute. He walked back to his fellow gang members. They were whispering about what to do with us.

Jimmy's and my prayer lives increased exponentially for those few minutes.

When they returned, the leader said, "We decided to let you guys stay for a while. We'll let the neighborhood know we talked with you. You'll be safe while you're here. The people around here could use some food. But when we say go, you go. And don't come back."

Jimmy and I responded, "Yes, sir. You are the boss. Thank you for letting us stay and feed everyone here."

I said, "My name is Art. What's yours?"

"That doesn't matter," he replied.

During the day, we met many young and old people who lived there. Some were friendly, and some were not, but they appreciated the food and drinks.

Many of the gang members walked up to us and revealed their scars where they had been shot. I wasn't sure if it was to impress or frighten us.

During our time there, we had some interesting conversations. We mainly heard, "Why did you guys come here and buy this food for us?"

Talk about God opening a door. There it was. We shared that Jesus wanted us to come and let them know He loves them. He provided everything today, not Jimmy or myself.

Whenever we handed someone a plate of food, we also gave him or her a New Testament.

Some received our response well, while some were wary. Their entire lives, they learned not to trust anyone. How could they not? In that culture, you never received anything from anyone unless that person got something in return. "Unconditional" was not a word they were familiar with.

There were still some who were angry because we were there. But others were open and listened to what Jimmy and I had to say.

Later in the afternoon, the gang leader told us we should leave, so we started packing everything up. I had one more thing to say to him before we left and found out his name was George.

I said, "George, do you remember when we arrived earlier, you told us not to come back? After seeing what we did today in your neighborhood, Jimmy and I hoped you might have changed your mind about us returning."

George replied, "Some of these people don't know where their next meal is coming from. You guys can come back."

Jimmy and I thanked him. This time, he shook our hands. It was evident that the Holy Spirit was moving and orchestrating all of this. Relationships were being formed. Observing and being a small part of God's work was a blessing. We needed to return soon to follow up and have more spiritual conversations.

As Jimmy and I drove back to his house, we discussed everything that had happened during the day and planned our next trip to George's neighborhood. After unloading the truck, Jimmy and I prayed, thanking the Lord for His divine protection and the friendships made.

***

I then got back home to spend time with my family. I missed them so much. They were my first ministry as a husband and a dad. Vicky had planned many fun things we could all do before my next return trip to Chicago. We spent a lot of quality time together. It was what we needed.

As I was packing and preparing to return to Chicago, Jerry, the youth pastor at our church asked if he could go with me this time. "Of course," I said. He had a heart for teenage youth—the age of many gang members.

During the flight, I briefed him about what we had been doing in Chicago. We arrived early enough in the day to grab some lunch, then rode the L-Train toward Cabrini.

As we entered the projects, some of the young men I had become friends with saw us. They were out throwing the football we had purchased for them.

"Art, who's your friend? Does he want to come join in?"

Jerry looked at me sadly and said, "A week ago, I messed up my shoulder. I can't even toss a piece of paper in a trashcan, but I don't want to turn them down. I have to try, at least."

Jerry told them about his injury but then said, "Guys, please let me try and throw the football anyway."

We prayed for Jerry and his shoulder. Then they handed him the football and started running some short routes. We couldn't believe it. Jerry was able to toss the ball about twenty yards.

They took off again and this time went out about thirty yards. Jerry threw a perfect spiral that distance. He continued throwing with the guys for another fifteen minutes. We just stared at each other in disbelief. This was really happening. The Lord answered our prayers. What a mighty God we serve.

We have all probably experienced this: When it seems like there is no hope, God's grace shows up. It certainly did that day.

After spending another hour with the guys, we returned to our room to discuss the day's events. I crinkled up a piece of paper and tossed it to Jerry. As he reached out to catch it, he let out a loud yell of pain. I asked him to toss it into the trashcan only a few feet away. He couldn't throw it that far.

We spent the next half hour praying and thanking God for His marvelous and powerful intervention. You can bet that our "faith-o-meter" rose substantially that day due to the miracle we saw.

The next day Jerry wanted to see the locations of some of the things I talked about in the past. After renting a car, we began to drive.

"This is where the young men threw me in the car and sped off to protect me," I said. "And this is the street corner that sold for a million dollars so a gang could be left alone to sell their drugs. Of course, that agreement didn't last very long." We kept driving, "This is the church where the young man was shot and killed as the result of a gang initiation. He was just leaving the church service, and the killer didn't even know him. Eyewitnesses said that after killing the young man, the shooter stepped over his body like he was a piece of meat. He began jumping up and down joyfully because he was now a gang member."

Jerry was shaken to hear how insignificant life is on the mean streets of Chicago. His heart and calling were for teenagers.

I said, "You know, Jerry, where people see dangerous gang members living a terrible lifestyle, we certainly don't make excuses for them. But God sees a potentially godly husband and father. He wants to break this violent generational cycle. The young people call us "suits." They won't get cleaned up and walk into a church to hear the gospel. We must go where they are and be Jesus' hands and feet."

"I agree."

As we continued to talk, Jerry said, "Art, I see you aren't wearing your gold wedding band. Is everything okay at home?"

I laughed. "Yes, my friend. Everything is fine with Vicky and me. We have a tradition we do each time I leave for Chicago. It isn't wise to wear shiny or valuable items into the projects. People get killed for less. Several years ago, when the ministry started, Vicky started taking my wedding band and wearing it on her thumb whenever I left for Chicago. Each time I return, she gives it back to me. This small act has become very precious to us both.

"That is beautiful, brother," Jerry said. "She is such an important part of the ministry."

"Yes, she is. When we are asked to speak at churches, conventions, or media, they want to hear her testimony rather than mine. She is always asked the same question: 'How have you been able to hold it together whenever Art leaves, not knowing if he will come back due to the danger?'"

Her answer is always the same. "At first, having him off doing the gang ministry was hard on me and our family. But it has also been a blessing because God has taught me not to hold on to things that don't belong to me. He belongs to God and must obey his calling."

"That is why she is my hero, Jerry," I replied.

The next day I asked Jerry to pray for me about something. After spending so many years on the streets with gangs, prostitutes, the homeless, and drug addicts, my heart started to become a little hard. Understandably, many would always approach me and start a conversation by saying, "God bless you." This is how they try to play a person to get something from them. I asked Jerry to please pray that my heart would not harden and that I would see people as Jesus did.

Jerry and I talked about a powerful story found in John 8:1–11 (ESV) regarding the woman caught in adultery. The religious leaders were testing Jesus, and the people wanted her stoned to death. When Jesus said, *"Let him who is without sin among you be the first to throw a stone at her,"* all her accusers walked away. Jesus asked her in verse 10, *"Woman, where are they? Has no one condemned you?"* In verse 11, she replied, *"No one, Lord." And Jesus said, "Neither do I condemn you; go, and from now on sin no more."*

Jerry and I talked about what a beautiful picture that was about Christ's love, compassion, and forgiveness for street people. May we have those same eyes as our Savior.

Jerry said that one of his favorite verses was Proverbs 4:23, *"Keep your heart with all vigilance, for from it flow the springs of life"* (ESV). Then he prayed for me immediately and promised to continue doing so.

We can't be effective in evangelism if we don't see people the way Jesus sees them.

Chapter 7

Gangs in Prisons

From the ride to the airport to the entire flight to Florida, Jerry and I discussed all we had experienced. It was such a blessing to be accompanied by someone who had a similar broken heart for the gangs and street people.

It was great to see my wife and kids again. After many hugs and kisses, rest, and time spent with Vicky and the kids, Vicky said she had an important message to give me from the assistant director of one of our area's juvenile lock-ups.

I called the number. I asked to speak with John, the man who had left the message.

"Art, thank you for returning my call. We don't know each other, but could we get together and discuss something the Lord has laid on my heart? The ministry you are involved in is just what our young men need. They are involved in gangs all over the state of Florida."

"Sure, John. Can we meet tomorrow for lunch?"

"That would be perfect, Art. I'll meet you at Wendy's near the facility at noon. See you then."

I wondered what this was all about. We aren't supposed to be ministering to gang members who are incarcerated, are we? Of course we are. I asked the Lord to forgive me for being so narrow-minded.

Vicky and I prayed for God to show us the direction He wanted His ministry to go. I had never considered this and thought Gang Rescue would always be ministering on the streets. We prayed and tried to keep an open mind for the meeting the next day.

After introductions and ordering our food, John got down to business.

"Art, I have worked with these angry and troubled young men for years. Being a follower of Christ, I'm convinced the only chance they have after being released is the power of God. Hearing what you guys have done in Chicago over the years, I know God's love and His Word need to be in this facility. As an employee, there are limitations on what I can do or say. But you and your team, through Christ, can offer them hope and a future. I only ask you to consider this. We can get you in here weekly or monthly, whatever you decide. Thanks for hearing my heart."

"John," I said, "your compassion and heart for these young men are inspiring and awesome. So is your faith. Please give our volunteers and me a little time to pray about and discuss this. I will get back to you. It has been a privilege and blessing to be with you today."

I told the ministry volunteers about the meeting. They promised to pray and let me know their thoughts. It would be a big commitment that we didn't want to take lightly. These young gang members had promises made and broken to them all their lives. We didn't want to do the same.

In a few days, I heard back from everyone. It was unanimous. They felt the Lord was leading the ministry in this direction too.

The decision was made, and I called John to let him know. We agreed that to be effective, we would need to go in every week. To say he was excited is an understatement. So were we.

John set up a time for me and the volunteers to go through some of the same training their guards underwent. I didn't know so many ordinary items could be used as weapons. We would be searched each time we entered the facility. That was mandatory for all prisons.

We decided to meet on Thursday evenings, which was good with the facility, and we would start the following week. Until then, everyone would pray for God's direction and guidance.

Thursday evening came, and we all checked in. There was to be one hour of Bible study each week. And no one knew what to expect.

After being ushered by the guards into the room where we were to meet, we waited for the young men to come in under guard. There were around eighty men in the facility. John told me they couldn't be forced to participate in the "service," so we had no idea how many to expect.

In a few minutes, the door opened, and in they came. As they took their seats, I recognized many of their gang tattoos from what I had seen in Chicago. About forty chose to come, or half of the facility.

There we so many that came, they put us in the dining hall. Everything in the room was made of steel and bolted to the floor so nothing could be taken or used as a weapon. As I looked out a window, I was reminded that we were in a prison by seeing the razor wire around the 12-foot-high fencing.

As the young men came in, their faces had looks of anger, frustration, and uncertainty. They were sizing us up as the guards yelled for them to sit down and be quiet. They weren't sure about us or our motives for being there.

John introduced us to the guys and gave them specific instructions to behave and respect our being there. He said, "Gentlemen, these people came here to be with you voluntarily. They left their families at home and don't get paid to do this. They are here because they care about you. I'll let them tell you why."

I started by saying, "Guys, there is no place we would rather be than with you. We work with young men who come from pasts and streets like yours. Let me ask you a question, and be honest. By raising hands, who in here believes God loves them?"

Only a couple of hands went up.

"Let me ask you another question. Be honest. Who in here believes if you were still on the streets right now, you would probably be dead?"

Most all of the hands went up.

I said, "I believe that proves God loves you. In His holy Word, Jeremiah 29:11 says, '*For I know the plans I have for you, declares the Lord, plans for welfare and not for evil, to give you a future and a hope'* (ESV). Guys, God doesn't break promises. My last question is, "Who here has a grandmother praying for you daily?"

Most of the hands went up again. "That's what I thought."

I could tell they didn't trust us yet, which was understandable. That would come with time as relationships began to grow.

"Men," I said, "let's spend the rest of our time in this first meeting just talking and getting to know each other better. We can start the Bible studies next week. We brought each of you a Bible to take back in your rooms and keep."

After our time of interaction, I said, "We want to end by saying one more thing that might make you uncomfortable. It is this: We love you guys. Jesus put that in our hearts. You have probably never heard a man tell you that before. We love you. Jesus loves you. See you next week."

The following week, Vicky, our thirteen-year-old son, Buddy, and I attended our church's Wednesday night service. Buddy loved the Lord with all his heart. His mother and I were so grateful.

At the end of the service, our pastor gave an invitation. And as we began to sing the first hymn, Buddy went forward and knelt at the altar. He was sobbing.

Vicky and I looked at each other bewildered. We knew he had been saved. He was also very shy and normally showed no emotions in public.

Vicky said, "You need to go up there, pray with him, and see if he is all right." Then she began to cry too. "I think I know why he went to the altar tonight."

Leaving my seat, I went forward and knelt beside Buddy. "Are you okay, son?"

"Dad, Jesus has called me to the gang ministry too. It isn't because you're my dad, and I want to do whatever you do. The Lord clearly and truly burdened my heart for gangs."

To say I was surprised is an understatement. Thinking about our son being on those dangerous streets I had walked for years frightened me. Vicky has always been discerning about things regarding God. I wondered why she had started crying when Buddy went forward. The Lord must have been speaking to her as well as to our son.

Kneeling together at the altar, "Buddy, I believe your mom knows why you came up tonight. When we go back to our seats, she will be crying. That doesn't mean she doesn't support your calling. She will just be acting like a loving mother."

We stood and returned to our seats. There she was, quietly sobbing. Many of the ladies in our church were hugging, consoling, and praying for her. I don't know what we would do without our church family.

After the service, we all went home. After Buddy had gone to bed, Vicky and I discussed what had happened.

She said, "Arthur, you know I would never try to interfere with God's plan and calling on any of our children. It has just been so hard, all these years, with you leaving to minister to the gangs in Chicago. I've always supported your calling and will forever. Neither you nor Buddy belong to me, and I will always support you in whatever the Lord calls you to. As a mother and wife, it is still so hard. I guess I just needed to have a little pity party for a while."

"Vicky, you have always been my hero in the faith. Your testimony about my belonging to God has inspired and encouraged many. With Buddy being called to the same dangerous ministry, I know it will be an even tougher burden for you. I believe the Lord knows whom He can trust to hold up. I promise to be in constant prayer for you. As you know, no one ever said serving God is easy, but the blessings far outweigh the hardships, as you have taught me."

That night we prayed for each other and our son. It is an honor to serve our Lord and Savior. As the old saying goes, "We don't know what the future holds, but we know Who holds the future."

***

It soon came time to return to Chicago. The wonderful ministry volunteers would keep the weekly prison ministry going in Florida.

God had opened another door the previous time I was in Chicago. A man named Pete lived in the building where I always stayed, and we became friends over the years as I traveled to and from Chicago. Pete grew up with a young man who became the leader of the Bloods gang in Chicago. The two men eventually took different paths in life but remained friends.

Pete had recently become aware of the type of ministry I was involved in. He told me about the relationship he had with his gang leader friend, Paco. "I don't spend much time with Paco anymore," he said. "It's too dangerous. But we're still friends. If you like, I can put in a good word for you and see if he'll meet with you. Where he and his gang live is a very violent and dangerous area, but I can try and hook you guys up."

"Pete," I replied, "that is what I'm here for. I would greatly appreciate it. Please let me know what he says."

As we all know, there are no accidents or coincidences with God. This was too great an opportunity to pass up.

A few days later, I ran into Pete in our building. He said, "I met with Paco, and he said he will meet with you. He also said there was no way he could guarantee your safety because of the many gang wars going on. The Bloods meet in an old abandoned warehouse on the south side. Here's the address. Be careful. Nearly every night, the news reports shootings and killings between the gangs in that part of town. For your safety, mention my name when you run into any of the gang members. Hopefully, that will be some help in getting you in. Paco said to come around 7:00 any Tuesday night."

I thanked Pete for his help and introduction. Then I called my family and church to pray about Tuesday night's meeting. Prayer is where the battle is first won.

On Tuesday I spent most of the day in prayer for God's protection and for relationships to be formed with the Bloods. Having studied the gang, I could expect them all to wear red. They were founded in 1972 and are a nationwide and international gang. Their main rivals have always been the Crips, whose color is blue.

As the 7:00 hour approached, I loaded my backpack with New Testaments—my sword. Taking the city bus got me fairly close to the address Pete gave me. I walked and prayed the rest of the way. Pete was right. It was a neighborhood devastated by poverty and violence. Bullet holes and graffiti were everywhere. Plywood replaced most of the windows that had been shot out. Most of the dilapidated buildings had been boarded up to try and keep the homeless and drug addicts out. The entire block looked like it had been deserted for decades. It was a depressing sight.

Arriving at the address, I saw the old run-down and abandoned warehouse Pete had described. As I neared the building, two young men wearing red were guarding the entrance. As I got closer, their hands moved down toward their waistbands. They laid their hands on the butts of their pistols, ready to act. I felt a lump in my throat, and beads of sweat dripped off my forehead. My mouth was completely dry. Thoughts of being home safely with my family raced through my mind.

One young man asked, "What are you doing here? Are you crazy? Are you tired of livin'? Are you lost?"

I couldn't get the words out of my mouth fast enough, "My name is Art. I'm a friend of Pete, and he is Paco's friend. I was told that Paco said it was okay for me to come and meet with him here any Tuesday around 7:00."

"What's in the backpack? Lift your hands. I'm going to search you."

I lifted my hands. "There are only Bibles in my backpack."

He searched me, then said, "Empty it so I can see."

After I emptied the backpack, he said, "Wait here."

As he entered the building, the other guy glared at me. "Don't you move."

I stood there praying and wondering how this would all turn out. It was easy to overhear the young man inside the building, telling Paco what I had said.

After what seemed like an eternity, the guard came out. "You can go in now."

What a relief as the tone of the young man's voice had become less threatening.

I put the Bibles back into my backpack and entered the building. The place was dimly lit, with several candles and one light bulb. The room had a stale odor of marijuana, alcohol, and urine. About twenty-five men sat on old, discarded chairs and sofas. In the middle of the area was a card table where five guys played dominos. They were all dressed in red, passing around joints and wine bottles. Weapons were everywhere. In addition to the pistols and automatic weapons, I spotted knives and machetes, too. It looked like they were ready for a war.

One of them at the card table looked at me "You Art, Pete's friend?"

"Yes, I am. Thanks for agreeing to see me."

Paco said, "The only reason you got in here is that Pete says you're okay. I don't know if you're smart, coming into this neighborhood alone, but I respect your guts. What do you want?"

"I know this might sound crazy to you guys," I answered. "But I want to prove that I care about you and your families. Hopefully, we can become friends, and I can earn your trust. I know talk is cheap, but as we get to know each other better, you will realize I don't have any bad motives. Will you guys give me a chance?"

Paco replied, "Art, some of our guys are unhappy with me because I let you in here. One of our boys you met out front says you're carrying a lot of religious books with you. You some preacher or church dude?"

"I'm not a preacher, but I do attend a church back home in Florida, where I live. I return to Chicago regularly and would like to spend more time with you guys if you let me."

Paco said they would talk about it and let me know through Pete.

Finally, I stated, "Before I leave tonight, would you men mind if I said a prayer for you and your families? We are all concerned about things in our lives, and God wants to hear them and help us. Maybe you have a sick child, an ailing grandmother, or a brother or sister getting into trouble. Is anyone against me praying before I leave?"

"Couldn't hurt," Paco said. "Anybody not want Art to pray? Don't look like it. Go ahead, Art."

I asked everyone to bow their heads and close their eyes. My prayer was for the young gang members' protection and their families. When we finished, I thanked them and started to leave. To my surprise, several young men walked up, thanked me, and shook my hand. I even got a few hugs, but most stayed back.

"Art, be careful as you leave," Paco said. "Bodies turn up around here all the time. A couple of our boys will escort you out of here for a short distance."

I got back on the bus and returned to my room, so grateful for my Heavenly Father's protection. He allowed me, again, to see there is nobody so hard that He can't reach.

Chapter 8

Locked Up but Free

My family and I missed each other so much. It had been eight years since my first venture to Chicago, and these many trips had taken a physical and emotional toll on all of us. Even so, the ministry caused our faith to grow stronger.

Vicky told me that what got her through was reading God's Word for hours every day. She also prayed for me and cried daily.

I asked how the kids had been doing lately.

"They have had highs and lows. One day, when they were exceptionally worried, I took them to talk to our pastor. He prayed with them and said he couldn't promise their daddy would return, but God would care for everyone. After that, they seemed to be fine. Children are so resilient, and I believe the Lord was covering them with strength and peace."

I was eager to hear from our volunteers how the services were going in the juvenile lock-ups. Praise God, it was good news. Relationships had formed, and several young men prayed to receive Christ. I was looking forward to going with everyone the next Thursday night.

Finally, that evening rolled around, and we all piled into a van to go and take God's Word behind the razor wire.

We were always thankful for the many who joined us each week. Initially, they were wary about what to expect. It's understandable, knowing the gangs and the family backgrounds they came from. Most never had a positive or loving male role model. That's where much of their anger came from. But our God is bigger than all that. We have seen Him change the lives of some of the young men.

One of the biggest blessings in our lives is when one of the guys walks over, hugs us, and says, "I love you." What a mighty God we serve.

I would never have thought the Lord would add to His street gang ministry by going into juvenile prisons too. His plans are always better than ours. We are just to trust and obey.

The volunteers who go are dedicated to the young gang members. They try not to miss a Thursday night because the inmates have always had promises made to them broken. Also, they have never had any consistency in their lives. The stakes are too high to start strong and fade away.

One evening I said, "Guys, we recently received a phone call from a young man who was released from this facility about a year ago. He wanted us to tell you to trust Jesus. Here is why. He said that while he was incarcerated, he was upset with God. He had been praying that the judge would sign his letter so he could go home. Instead, his release date kept being pushed back. In his frustration, he thought the Lord must not care. Later, his release papers were signed, and he went back home to his neighborhood. In his neighborhood is a street corner where he and his best friend always hung out. He found that during the time he was still locked up, his buddy was killed in a drive-by shooting. He went on to say that if he had been released when he wanted to be, he would no doubt be dead too. He also said, 'Art, tell the guys in there to trust God. His plans and timing are perfect. The Lord truly is loving and caring.'"

After hearing that story, the room became very quiet.

We never know what our heavenly Father is up to. One evening, at the end of the Bible study, Clint, one of our volunteers, gave an invitation to be saved. We looked around the room to see if anyone was coming forward. To our surprise, a guard came forward. That was a blessing to us and an example to the young men.

***

As time passed, the Lord called two ladies to go to the facility with us. They were both grandmothers in their eighties. If any of these guys had a family member in their lives, it was usually a grandmother. Many times, while the Bible study was going on, we would see one of the grandmothers sitting between two of the guys holding their hands. The boys loved them.

One evening, I was looking across the room to be sure everything was going okay between the inmates and the volunteers. One of the grandmothers was crying. Oh no, I thought. What did one of the guys say to her that was inappropriate?

I ran to the table where they were sitting. "Maxine, what happened? What is wrong?"

"Art, I was holding his hand and praying with him. When we finished, he said he had forgotten how warm a grandmother's hand felt."

Hearing this brought tears to my eyes too. I felt ashamed for judging the young man and thinking the worst. Blessings came in so many ways.

The next week, as we were entering the facility and being searched, one of the guards asked if he could speak to me in private. We went into a side room, and he said, "One inmate wants to attend the Bible study. His name is Spike, and he claims to be a Satan worshipper. He also told some of his buddies that he wanted to try to disrupt the service. We hesitated to allow him to attend. What do you think?"

"Yes, please bring him in. We want him there, and I am sure God does too. Thanks for telling me."

As we were all being escorted to the room by a guard, I alerted the volunteers about this, and then we prayed specifically that this young man would receive Christ. We also prayed that he would not be allowed to disrupt the Bible study.

As the guards brought them all in, the guard who warned me earlier quietly pointed out the young man, and I passed the information on to the volunteers.

As the greetings, handshakes, and hugs went on, I approached the young man and said, "Hi, Spike. You do not know how glad I am that you joined us. You might think that your coming in here was your idea. But it was God who brought you to this service because He loves you. I love you too. And I believe He has something to say to you tonight."

As I walked away, Spike had a confused look on his face. We continued to pray for him during the study, and the guards watched him closely.

It was my turn to lead the lesson that day, and I started by asking the young men to look around the room. "In the future, some of you will receive Christ as your Savior and have a wonderful life. That doesn't mean you won't have tough times, but Jesus will be there to help you through them. Some of you will not want to change, and you'll end up in the Big House (adult prison). And finally, it hurts me to say this, some of you will end up dead because you wouldn't trust Jesus and leave the gang lifestyle." I then told them to open their Bibles to Jeremiah 29:11 because this verse reveals God's heart. "As I said, that doesn't mean we won't have problems if we accept Jesus as our Savior. But we can still have joy, hope, and peace because He will walk with us through it all."

Then we turned to Joshua 24:15 (ESV). *"And if it is evil in your eyes to serve the LORD, choose this day whom you will serve, whether the gods which your fathers served in the region beyond the River, or the gods of the Amorites in whose land you dwell. But as for me and my house, we will serve the LORD."*

We discussed how tomorrow is a day found only on a fool's calendar. We are not promised tomorrow.

Then one of the volunteers gave the invitation. It was humbling and a blessing to see two young men come forward. And one of them was Spike. The Satan-worshipper. The one who had wanted to disrupt the lesson. What a mighty God we serve.

The volunteers who went to the facility each week came from various backgrounds. One man, Jon, was a former Force Recon Marine. Before that, in his youth, he had been locked up in a facility much like the one we were in. During his incarceration, a Christian motorcycle group visited that jail and shared their testimonies about coming to know Jesus. That was when Jon became a believer. He is a devoted follower of Christ and has a tender heart toward these young men. They listen when he tells them that being incarcerated was the greatest blessing of his life because that is when he was saved.

The Lord continued to grow this, His ministry. As other juvenile lock-up directors heard about the Bible studies, they wanted to bring them to their facilities.

Before we knew it, God added four more facilities to the one we were going to. It spread the volunteers thin, but how could we say no?

We were now in four men's facilities and one for young ladies. Most of the girls had been in gangs also. And God continued to bring in more dedicated volunteers to handle the busy schedule. Due to God's perfect plan, He brought together a wonderful team of volunteers with different strengths and gifts. Some had the gift of evangelism and were excellent communicators as they delivered the messages each week. Others were awesome prayer warriors as they prayed for salvation decisions during the lesson. Many were gifted with building one-on-one relationships with the young men. They were all faithful to the Great Commission whatever abilities the Lord gave them. We began seeing many get saved.

While this all was happening, I was to return to Chicago in a couple of weeks. We didn't want much time to pass between the occasions we met with those we had built relationships with. They still needed encouragement to stand firm in their faith. Also, God kept opening more doors to share the good news in other city areas.

***

The day arrived for me to fly to Chicago. My family and I were praying together as the cab pulled up. We hugged, kissed, and cried as I prepared to leave. As usual, Vicky took my wedding band and put it on her thumb until I returned. And while on the flight, as usual, I asked the Lord to guide my steps in Chicago according to His will and for His glory alone. The cheap hotel where I usually stayed now seemed like a second home after all these years.

After being away for a few weeks, there was always concern that some of the gang members I had gotten close to might have been killed.

As soon as I entered the projects, several guys I knew frantically ran up to me "Art, Wishbone's been shot. He's in the hospital and has been asking for you."

My heart sank. "Is he going to be okay?"

"He was shot three times, but they think he's going to make it."

"Okay, guys. You be praying for him. I'm going to catch a cab and get to the hospital."

The taxi ride seemed to take forever. Wishbone was a young man who had prayed to be saved only a few months earlier.

The lady at the front desk also said he had been asking for me. "He is a lucky young man. The bullets didn't penetrate any vital organs. Here is our map of the hospital with instructions on how to get to his room. He has been out of ICU for two days."

Thanking her, I took off to find Wishbone.

I tapped on the door and went in. He had all kinds of tubes and IVs attached, along with a lot of bandages. My biggest fear was that Wishbone might question God and his faith after this happened to him.

When Wishbone saw me, a big smile came across his face. "Art, you made it. Thanks for coming. God is still good." Hearing him say those words instantly relieved my concerns. I choked up a bit.

As best as I could, without pulling any of the tubes out, we gave each other a big hug "As soon as I heard what happened, I came as fast as possible."

An older lady was sitting in the corner of the room. "Art, this is my grandma, Nellie. Grandma, this is the man I've been telling you about. He is the guy that prayed with me to accept Jesus as my Savior."

I walked across the room and embraced her. "What a pleasure meeting you, Ms. Nellie. I'm sorry it is under these circumstances."

"No, Art. It is my pleasure to meet you. My grandson told me you have been bringing God's Word into Cabrini. Those young men are caught up in that terrible gang life. You are an answer to my prayers. My grandson was pulled into that life, initially for protection from other gangs. I am a Christian. He isn't a bad boy. His environment has pulled him down. I know that his only true hope is Jesus. I cry myself to sleep every night, praying he won't be killed. Look at him. He was shot in the leg, side, and shoulder. I believe the Lord is giving him another chance."

"Ms. Nellie, I honestly believe that a lot of these young gang members are still alive today because of the precious prayers of their grandmothers."

Wishbone said, "Art, the doctors said I should get out in about two weeks. Then there'll be some time for me to heal up. My grandma will help with that."

"I sure will," Ms. Nellie chimed in. "Art, after my grandson is released, would you come to my apartment so we could cook you a meal?"

"I wouldn't miss it, Ms. Nellie. I'll also be back here to check on him. Before I leave, may I say a prayer for you both?"

"Please do, Art,"

We prayed together for Wishbone to heal and recover. I also prayed for strength for Nellie as she would nurse him back to health. Finally, we thanked God that Wishbone was still alive after being shot three times.

Chapter 9

The Angels Were Rejoicing

The next day I met with some of the guys in Cabrini to continue our weekly Bible study. When I say weekly, I mean the weeks I'm in Chicago rather than Florida. It amazed me that the number of young gang members who came grew so large. I could see the spiritual tug-of-war going on. Some were glad I was there, while others would have nothing to do with me. The enemy didn't like anyone trying to take away people or territory that belonged to him.

Later, as I was walking through the projects, a man was riding his bicycle. He kept circling and staring at me. I was going to dismiss it as just his being another street person with some mental challenges. Then suddenly, he started coming way too close. Eventually, he stopped his bike next to me, still staring as if I were the only one there.

I am normally more aware of my surroundings, but I hadn't noticed he had a machete in a sheath tied to his bicycle. Now the situation felt a bit more serious. The hair on the back of my neck stood up, as it did my arms. My mouth became dry, and all my senses were on alert.

Was this guy dangerous or just not all there? I wasn't going to give him the benefit of the doubt, so I took a few steps back. What he did next made my skin crawl and my knees go weak. He pulled the machete from the sheath, pointed it toward the sky, and started chanting some gibberish. I was caught off guard, not knowing whether to fight or run.

Then, a short distance from where this was happening, I saw three young men I knew running toward me. When they arrived, one took the machete from the man and slid it back into the sheath. The other two yelled at the guy to go and move on.

Crazy situation handled.

"Thanks, guys," I said. "What was that all about? What is that dude's story?"

"He's been around here for a long time. Nobody knows much about him. Rumors are that he's some spiritual nut job. Some say he's even killed people and dumped their bodies where no one can find them. The bottom line is that we didn't want him messing with you. A lot of strange things have happened in Cabrini over the years. Things people haven't been able to explain. You okay, Art?"

"Yes, guys. Thanks to you. I appreciate you coming to my rescue."

"No problem, Art. We got your back."

***

By then I had been in Chicago for a few weeks and needed to return home to my family. I also wanted to see how the ministry at the juvenile prisons was going. I flew back to Niceville and spent desperately needed quality time with my family.

We had been bringing God's Word to the five youth facilities for about four years by now. Many had been saved and wanted to be baptized. We counted them: thirty. It was humbling as well as a blessing to hear. If we baptized that many in our church, there would be no time for a sermon.

The next day I called our pastor and asked if it would be possible to use the baptistry in our church. "Maybe we could have the baptisms on a day other than Sunday. You wouldn't have time to baptize all thirty and give a sermon too."

"Art," he said, I believe we need to do this on a Sunday. It would be important for our people to see because this is what we should all be about."

"Thank you. Whatever you want to do it is great. I have already received permission from the facility director, who is a believer, and they will have plenty of guards to bring the guys." All of the detailed plans were set. The baptisms would happen in three weeks. The director wanted to send invitations to all of the family members across the state.

I told the director we knew many families couldn't afford the gas to get to the event. We said the ministry would happily send gas cards to families who needed them.

The three weeks passed, and that Sunday was here. As the families arrived, our church members warmly greeted them. They came from as far away as Miami, Tampa, West Palm Beach, and Jacksonville.

He began, "The Scriptures tell us in Luke 15:10 that all the angels in heaven rejoice over just one who comes into the family of God. Can you imagine the party they are having right now? Welcome, families. Let's get started."

The baptisms began. Many times, when an inmate's name was called and he was baptized, the family members cried and praised God. By the time all thirty were baptized, there wasn't a dry eye in the sanctuary. Many families traveled long distances to see their son or grandson baptized. We had sent gas cards to most of the families because they couldn't afford to buy the gas to get here. But they were not about to miss this special event. Many waved handkerchiefs and shouted "Praise God" as their loved ones were baptized. It was such a special and joyous time.

At the end, the pastor said, "I was thinking about delivering an abbreviated message today, but I have changed my mind. Today we have witnessed a much more powerful sermon than I could ever deliver. Seeing all of these young men baptized is a sermon in itself. Due to their incarceration, I know many of the family members haven't seen them in a while. We have a reception with some desserts and refreshments in our fellowship hall. Let's meet there together so you can be reunited for a little while before they return to the facility. Everyone is welcome."

I can't describe in words. The young men and their families hugged and cried, as did our members. The guards enjoyed themselves too. Only God could pull off something like this. I introduced our dedicated volunteers who go to the facilities each week, and thanked the Lord as we said a special prayer for them. God had worked powerfully through them in these young men's lives.

The ministry was now bringing God's Word into five juvenile lock-up facilities. Most of the young men and women in those facilities were in gangs from all over the state. What is truly sad is that as our country's basic family unit has been disintegrating. States can't build these facilities fast enough to keep up their need.

We learned early on that the female facility was very different from the ones for males. There were unique issues and challenges. In addition to the majority coming from extreme poverty and gang life, most had been emotionally and sexually abused. As a result, when we read and talked about God the Father, many were repulsed by the word "father." At times, while we were conducting a Bible study there, a young lady would stand up and start screaming. All the other girls would run over and comfort her. The staff and guards told us the sudden outburst was because she was having a flashback of a horrible experience. It was heartbreaking.

But because of our Lord and Savior, all hope is not lost for these precious, hurting young ladies. I thought about Luke 4:18–19 (ESV) when Jesus quoted Isaiah 61:1, *"The Spirit of the Lord is upon me, because He has anointed me to proclaim good news to the poor. He has sent me to proclaim liberty to the captives and recovering of sight to the blind, to set at liberty those who are oppressed, to proclaim the year of the Lord's favor."*

These verses apply to all of us who are followers of Christ.

We have seen many of the inmates be healed by the power and love of God. Some have gone from depression and hopelessness to peace and joy. It is amazing to see the Lord transform lives. Watching 2 Corinthians 5:17 come to fruition is a blessing. It says, *"Therefore, if anyone is in Christ, he is a new creation. The old has passed away; behold, the new has come"* (ESV).

We see so much in these facilities that hurts our hearts. They have experienced being abandoned by some of their family members. They have been told words like, "You will never amount to anything" and "I wish you were dead." Hearing things like this caused their self-worth to be destroyed, and anger to rise up inside them. The terrible stories go on and on.

The good news is that we have a Savior who can turn all of this around. He can heal all of this trauma, anger and harm. We have seen him do it through the power of his love.

One day as the girls were coming in for the Bible study, I saw that one inmate was pregnant. She looked so young. I asked one of the staff members about her story. It turns out that she was fourteen years old and impregnated by her uncle. When I was told this, anger rose up inside me toward that man. I don't know if the emotion that came over me was righteous indignation or sin, but it's what I felt as a dad. If something like that happened to one of my daughters, I shutter to think what my reaction would be. I suppose that, as fathers, our flesh tends to well up inside us, but I pray that my reaction would be according to God's will and that he would be glorified.

A couple of weeks later, we invited a young Air Force officer to come and speak to the young ladies. She had a powerful testimony that we thought would truly impact the girls.

She said, "I have been looking forward to sharing my story with you young ladies because it is yours, too. I come from where most of you come from and have experienced what most of you have experienced."

She had their undivided attention.

She continued, "By the time you have heard about my past, you won't be able to say, 'You don't know what I have been through.' I love you ladies and want you to have the peace, joy, and hope I now have. This uniform, with the captain bars, might make you think I have always had it all together. That is not the case."

You could hear a pin drop in the room as the inmates' eyes and ears were riveted on the captain's every word.

She continued "I came from a fairly good family. When I turned fifteen, I decided to leave home and go out on my own. Having no money or income, I prostituted myself on the streets to be able to buy food. A pimp, whom I thought was my boyfriend, got me hooked on drugs. Later he started to physically and sexually abuse me. He thought I was his personal property. My life kept spiraling downhill and was out of control. One night I overdosed and nearly died. I'm still not sure if that happened accidentally or on purpose. Finally, I was caught robbing a convenience store, arrested, and locked up in a place like where you are now. Believe it or not, that was the greatest blessing of my life."

That last statement she made caused the girls to have looks of confusion on their faces. How could being locked up be a good thing?

She then asked them a question, "Be honest. How many of you believe if you weren't locked up right now but were back on the streets, that you could be dead?"

The majority of the young ladies' hands went up. She was being honest with them, and they were honest with her.

She said, "While locked up, I realized God loved me. He put me in a safe place, made sure I had food and a bed to sleep in, and most importantly, brought people in, as you have here, to share God's Word with me. The Bible gave me encouragement and much more. It says His desire is not to harm us but to give us hope and a future. Unlike many people we have known, God doesn't break promises. He promises to walk with us daily through the good and the tough times. God also promises to fight our battles if we just trust Him. He loves us and is a good Father. Eventually, I prayed to accept Jesus as my personal Savior, and have not looked back since. Sometimes I go through difficult times, but He is always with me and gets me through to the other side."

Some of the girls began to sob as the Holy Spirit worked on their hearts.

She concluded, "Ladies, the greatest decision you can ever make is to pray to receive Jesus as your personal Savior. You may think you need to get your life cleaned up first. That is not how it works. He wants us to come just as we are. Christ will do the work in us. It is called salvation, and it can't be earned because it is a gift. Who in here today would like to pray and receive that gift?"

Fifteen hands rose up. As we prayed with the young ladies, we all had tears flowing. Even some of the staff and guards were "leaking."

After we were finished, the captain said, "Let me end with this. After what most of us here have been through, people say we are "cutters." That means we try to get the internal pain out by cutting ourselves. I want to show you something."

She pulled up her sleeves to show them the scars on her arms from the past. The girls pulled up their sleeves to show her the scars on their arms.

She said, "These scars now represent our victory in Christ because of where He brought us from. Don't be ashamed of them, but show your scars to others. Use them as you share your testimony to help others."

The girls mobbed her with hugs, kisses, and tears when she finished. They had a lot of questions, which she graciously stayed to answer. All glory to God.

After we had been going to the juvenile facilities for quite some time, I asked if we could have cookouts at each of them once a year and bring some sports equipment. The directors approved, and we were glad to add this activity to the Bible studies.

We decided to have the first cookout at the young ladies' facility. After pulling the grill onto the grounds, some volunteers began kicking soccer balls, playing basketball, and tossing a football with the girls. Others talked one-on-one with several of the young ladies. One of the inmates, who was sixteen, started a conversation with us. She wanted to attend the University of Florida because she loved the Gators. We asked about her background, and her response broke our hearts.

"My name is Sally. I'm from Orlando. My father left us a few days after I was born. I guess he didn't want me. Our family was very poor, so my mother sent me out on the streets as a prostitute. She said I couldn't return home unless I brought at least $300.00 every night. It was a tough way to grow up."

The volunteers and I were in tears We couldn't help but hug her.

She continued, "I know God loves me and has a good plan for the rest of my life. He always protected me because there were times when any of the johns could have killed me."

We were speechless as this precious girl was ministering to us. She taught us a lot that day, and I'm sure she will become a Florida Gator.

While driving home after the cookout, thoughts ran through my mind about these young gang members and where they came from. I recalled the father-daughter dances our church held each year around Valentine's Day. These incarcerated young girls never had a chance to experience anything like that. They come from what we call "hell on earth." Their lives have been filled with physical, verbal, and sexual abuse. When we are asked to speak at churches, conference, and other meetings, when the audiences hear things like this, they are shocked. This is a world that most of them are sheltered from.

I thought about how my son and I went on camping trips and that we supported him and were there to watch his sporting events. Recently, our church had a Father-Son Day, where my grandsons and I made gingerbread houses. Most of these young people in the facilities either didn't know who their father was, or he was dead or in prison. I have a hard time using the word father in these cases. Life is so unfair.

But then my thoughts turned toward the Lord and all the young people in similar circumstances He had rescued and changed. After being released, sometimes, years later, we heard from someone who had been locked up. Some said they were married and took their families to church every Sunday. A few told us the Lord called them to be counselors to young people with backgrounds like theirs.

Over the years, we have learned that the Lord, even though he didn't cause traumatic events to happen, uses those past situations to help and heal others. He does this through his followers. When the abused person can't say, "You don't know what I have been through," he or she tends to listen much better to someone with the same experiences.

Chapter 10

Emergency Call from Chicago

I wasn't planning on returning to Chicago for two more weeks. Those plans changed when I received a telephone call.

A young gang member from Cabrini, whom we prayed with to be saved two months earlier, had been shot and killed. His name was Stitch, and he was faithful to the Bible studies there. This news was very disheartening because he had been in the process of turning his life around. Sadly, in the gang culture it is hard to overcome a past reputation. Generally, gang members know who are in rival gangs by reputation. Also, gangs know where their own territories begin and end, and they protect those boundaries violently.

Stitch's grandmother, brother, and sister wanted him to have a Christian funeral because he was a believer. They weren't affiliated with any church, so the family asked if I would conduct the service and burial.

Having never officiated at a funeral, I called our pastor to ask if it would be appropriate for a layman to act in this capacity.

"Art, I see nothing wrong with this. You have my blessing. I will be praying for you and the family."

I thanked him and called Stitch's brother back and asked when the funeral would be.

"We wanted the service on Friday, three days from now. We already have the location and plot. Thanks, Art. You have meant a lot to him and our family."

I needed to hurry and book a flight to Chicago. I let my family and our ministry volunteers know my plans. Vicky and everyone were very nervous about this trip. We all knew about the danger involved in attending a gang funeral. Those events are where many drive-by shootings occur. If rival gangs hear about it, they consider it an opportunity to have their enemies gathered in one place. More drive-buys happen at funerals than most other events, and the result is always numerous injuries and deaths.

I was nervous about it too. But there was no way I would disappoint Stitch's family.

Friday arrived, and even before I left for the airport, our volunteers were still trying to talk me out of going. I thanked them for their concern and asked for their prayers. I kissed Vicky and the kids goodbye.

After checking into the hotel and resting a bit, I handed the taxi driver the address Stitch's brother had given me.

"Are you sure this is where you want to go?" the cabbie asked.

"Yes, sir."

"Okay. But I will not wait around for you. When I drop you off, I'm outta there. It isn't a very desirable neighborhood."

"No problem. I can catch a ride with someone after the funeral."

"Funeral, huh? Well, I hope it isn't yours. Those are some violent streets in there."

"Thank you, sir. I hope not, too."

Stitch's family told me it would only be about a block's walk from the road to the cemetery. Nearing the graveyard, I heard a lot of commotion and noise. It looked like there were over one hundred attending, Stitch's family and mostly his gang members.

"There's Art!" several young men yelled as I approached.

Walking toward the casket, I found Stitch's family members and hugged them. "I'm so sorry this happened. You have my prayers as well as my love. Stitch was a dear friend."

Since I knew most of the young men there because of my time spent in Cabrini, I also walked through the crowd to greet them.

At most gang funerals most gang members bring bottles of wine and have been drinking well before the service begins. In this case they loudly shouted Stitch's name to memorialize him. At some funerals, they fire their weapons into the air. It is a raucous and noisy event instead of the quiet and somber services most of us are familiar with.

To begin the service, I went to where the casket and family were and asked everyone to gather quietly.

Then I began. "We are all here today to mourn together, to celebrate together, and to honor the life of Stitch, whom we all loved. When his family called me where I live in Florida, it broke my heart to hear of his passing. Some of you know Stitch had prayed to receive Christ as his Savior. His request, if anything happened to him, was to have a Christian funeral. It is an honor for me to conduct his service. We will all miss him, but we can celebrate today because we know he is in heaven with Jesus. God's Word tells us that in heaven, there is no more pain, no more tears, and no more suffering.

"I know some of you in the crowd have also prayed that prayer, and you have the same hope, joy, and confidence Stitch had. He wanted you, his friends, to have the same opportunity to hear the gospel and accept Jesus as your Savior."

Opening God's Word, I read several verses from the book of Romans telling how a person can be saved. At the end of the service, I said, "If any of you would like to talk about this more, meet me tomorrow around 1:00 p.m. near the entrance to Cabrini."

Before leaving, I prayed again with the family. When the service ended, they kindly drove me back to my building.

Upon entering my room, I knelt and thanked God for His protection during Stitch's service. No drive-by shooting. The next day I would have an opportunity to share the good news. Then I called Vicky to tell her the service was over, and I was safe.

That evening as I was having my quiet time, I thought about the fact that in our society, gangs are outcasts. Many people think they can't be reached or changed. My thoughts also went to the outcasts of society in Jesus' day. To him, there were no outcasts. He spent most of His time with those rejected by the populous.

I thought about the shepherds in Luke 2:8–20. Society looked down on them because they were considered unclean due to their work with animals. Yet the announcement of Jesus' birth came to them.

I thought of the demon-possessed man in Luke 8:26–39 who was naked and lived among the tombs.

The people avoided him, but Jesus traveled to him and cast out the demons.

I thought about the Samaritan woman at the well, found in John 4:7–42. Here is another account of Jesus connecting with a societal reject. Jews did not associate with or speak to Samaritans, but Jesus did. As a result, she and many in her town believed and were transformed.

I thought of the lepers who had to yell, "Unclean!" whenever anyone came near them. People ran from them, but Jesus touched and healed them.

There are many other places in God's Word where Christ stopped to heal and to help. To God, there are no "throw-away" people. What a different world it would be if we saw people the way Jesus sees them. I am so thankful the Lord answered my prayer many years earlier and broke my heart for "the least of these." Maybe that is why I have such peace being on the streets with the gangs, homeless, drug addicts, and prostitutes. I really don't know, but pray that I would continue to have the same heart in the future.

I woke up the next morning, excited to share the gospel with the young men at the funeral who wanted to hear more. Four of the guys said they would show up, but nine came.

I shared my testimony and then read God's Word about how a person can be saved. I told how the Lord had mercy and forgave me for the sins I had committed in my younger days.

One of the young men said, "Art, I thought you always had it together."

I said, "None of us have it all together until we go home to be with Jesus. We should grow in our faith after being saved, but we never 'arrive' until we reach heaven. God's Word tells us in 1 John 1:8, *"If we say we have no sin, we deceive ourselves, and the truth is not in us"* (ESV).

After spending time together in the Bible, I gave an invitation. Four of the nine young men prayed to receive Christ as their Savior. It was very humbling to watch the Holy Spirit moving in the hearts of these gang members. Distributing New Testaments to all nine, I asked them to read some every day, and later we could discuss what they read.

When we finished, I left Cabrini and started toward the L-Train. A man approached me and asked if I would pray for him. He said, "I noticed how you've been sharing God's Word with folks around here over the years. I'm a Christian and haven't approached you before because I have aids. Most people run away from me when they hear that. But I know God can do anything."

He was carrying a backpack and showed me his Bible inside.

I replied, "You are right, my friend. There is nothing God can't do. My name is Art. What's yours?"

"My name is Paul."

"It would be an honor to pray with you, Paul. May I put my arm around your shoulder as we pray?"

"Sure, Art. That would be fine."

Paul and I stood in the middle of that sidewalk in downtown Chicago and prayed for each other. Surprisingly, as we prayed, several people who were walking by stopped to bow their heads. What a blessing.

When we finished, we hugged each other. I noticed Paul had tears in his eyes. He said, "Art, this is the first time anyone has touched me in several years. Thank you."

Hearing those words broke my heart and brought tears to my eyes too.

We exchanged telephone numbers and vowed to get together regularly.

***

It was time for me to fly back home. But first, I went back to Cabrini to tell everyone I would return in a few weeks. After spending a few hours there, I began walking toward the L-Train.

While walking, a guy came up and walked beside me.

"Is there something I can do for you?" I asked.

"I would surely like a cup of coffee."

"There's a coffee shop about a block ahead. I would be glad to buy you some coffee, my friend."

He asked, "What do you have in your backpack?"

"I keep some Bibles in it if anyone wants one. Here is one for you to keep. My name is Art. What's yours?"

"My name is Vince. I live on the streets but am trying to get my life back on track."

I bought each of us a cup of coffee and asked if he needed anything else, expecting him to ask for money.

"Art, can I ask you for one more thing?"

"What would you like?" I reached for my wallet.

"Would you please say a prayer for me? I've noticed you doing that for other people in the neighborhood.

I felt ashamed for assuming what I did about Vince and asked both him and God to forgive me.

We took each other's hands, and when I began praying, he knelt on the sidewalk there in front of all the people walking and driving by. It was difficult to continue praying as I choked back sobs. We hugged, and I thanked Vince for teaching me what I needed to learn that day.

We parted ways, and I checked out of the hotel. On the cab ride to Midway, I glanced out the taxi's window. There he was. To my dismay, Vince was at a convenience store, rummaging through a trashcan, trying to find something to eat.

My heart sank, and a lump rose in my throat. Why hadn't I done more for Vince? Vowing to find him on my next trip, I said to myself, "Maybe this is God's way of showing me the work He called me to in Chicago isn't yet finished."

EPILOGUE

A lot of things have happened since the ending of this book. The city government got their way, and Cabrini Green was torn down to the dismay of many of the previous residents. Many of the former gang members whose lives had been touched by God, moved out of the city with their families to have a fresh start. Silent moved out of state to live with family. Steven and his family moved to a city in southern Illinois to begin their lives again. There are many other examples of gang members moving far away from Chicago. I even heard where some started taking their families to church in their new locations.

    Little did we know the Lord was already at work to show us where he wanted Gang Rescue Ministries to go next. I will give you a hint. It was in Central America, and he would do some powerful things there, too. But that is another story for another time. Stay tuned . . .

About the Author

Art Wilson was born in Benton, Askansas and met his wife, Vicky, in Harrison, Arkansas. After marriage, the couple settled in Niceville, Florida, a small town on the Florida panhandle. They have three children and four grandchildren.

Made in the USA
Columbia, SC
30 March 2025